Praise for *AUTHENTIC FRATERNITY: The Notion of Fraternitas in Pope Benedict XVI's Caritas in Veritate and Africae Munus*

This masterpiece by Nkadimeng is a true reflection of Pope Benedict XVI's communion ecclesiology expressed through *Caritas in Veritate*, the fraternity or brotherhood that sticks together during the critical and challenging times. It is a clear contribution towards a thorough understanding of *Fraternitas*, Pope Benedict XVI's *Caritas in Veritate* and *Africae Munus*, as the tools towards cohesive and harmonious coexistence of humanity synergizing towards development guided by the principles of charity and truth. Nkadimeng unravels the theme of fraternity in socio-cultural and economic realities, pointing out that Benedict's magisterial teaching revolves around this theme.

This is a remarkable elucidation of the foundation of fraternity incorporating systematic theology, covering themes such as the triune God, Christology, ecclesiology, Sacramentology, anthropology, and eschatology. These dictums combine to effect pastoral theology and political theologies. Nkadimeng points out that these themes are prevalent in the encyclical and that they are incorporated into *Africae Munus* which is addressed to the Catholic community not only in Europe but also in Africa. The fourth chapter specifically deals with this that *Africae Munus* relates to *Caritas in Veritate* as applied in the work of reconciliation, justice and peace in the troubled continent of Africa. African narratives within political and social environments uncover the love of Christ, revealing a new brotherhood of love and truth created for the integral human development.

Dr. Kelebogile Resane
University of the Free State, South Africa

Erudite, thoughtful, and tackling some of the most important issues facing Christianity and the international community today – globalization, inculturation, development – this book analyzes Pope Benedict XVI's thought to show us an important political theology: one which understands that true human flourishing, whether in the African nations or elsewhere, cannot exist simply on a material level but needs to possess a holistic dimension that considers the spiritual development and fraternal well-being of the human person, recognizing the God-given dignity of being made in the Divine image and how ultimate fulfillment cannot avoid the nourishment of the soul. Other modern-day prophets, from Solzhenitsyn to St. John Paul II, have highlighted this message. The author delves into Benedict's thought, expounding on its deep insights while transcending uncritical admiration with a healthy articulation to what more is needed in the robust relationship between Christianity and Africa, making for an authentic African Christianity that is true to the sacred and moral doctrines of Catholicism while remaining sensitive to the dignity of local cultures, making the important distinction between receiving the faith versus receiving Westernization through an imposition of cultural colonialism. It is a struggle that the European nations also need to be sensitive to in the age of globalism: the battle to be rooted in the rich identity of one's national heritage while safeguarding universal fraternity. This masterful work makes an important contribution to these and ongoing conversations on moral, spiritual, and economic development, making central the importance of the Queen of the sciences in the discourse, thus the need for a political theology. This is an important and fascinating book, written with an intellectual's mind and a pastor's heart that makes a significant contribution; reminiscent of the works of the great political theologians writing today, from Stanley Hauerwas to William T. Cavanaugh, I highly recommend the work of Fr. Thabang Nkadimeng, a fresh, new voice in the field.

Fr. Daniel-Maria Klimek
Adjunct Professor
Saint Meinrad Seminary and School of Theology
Author of *Medjugorje and the Supernatural* (Oxford 2018) and
For the Love of Mary (Emmaus 2023)

AUTHENTIC FRATERNITY

The Notion of *Fraternitas* in Pope Benedict XVI's *Caritas in Veritate* and *Africae Munus*

By
Izrael Thabang Nkadimeng

CASA LAGO PRESS

Fuori Collana
Volume 2

The books in this series are of subject matter related to things Italian and/or Italian/American though not always in a direct manner. Hence, this "out of network" series allows Casa Lago Press to include subject matter "indirectly" related to the main mission of the Press.

The publication of this book has been made possible through a generous grant from an anonymous donor who wishes not to be identified but urges others to donate to historical and cultural studies.

This book was originally submitted to fulfill the thesis requirement for the licentiate degree in Systematic Theology at the Catholic University of America in Washington, DC. The thesis was approved by Chad C. Pecknold, Ph.D., as Director, and by Christopher Ruddy, Ph.D. as Reader.

ISBN 978-1-955995-17-7
Library of Congress Control Number: Available upon request

© 2025 Izrael Thabang Nkadimeng

All rights reserved.
Printed in the United States of America

CASA LAGO PRESS
New Fairfield, CT

TABLE OF CONTENTS

Foreword by Wilton Cardinal Gregory ... ix

Introduction ... 1

Chapter One. The Purpose and Method of *Caritas in Veritate* ... 5

Chapter Two. *Fraternitas* ... 25

Chapter Three. *Fraternitas* in Relation to Human Development ... 52

Chapter Four. The Notion of *Fraternitas* in *Africae Munus* ... 72

Chapter Five. Critical Comments on the Encyclical ... 100

Conclusion ... 112

Bibliography ... 114

Index ... 119

About the Author ... 121

Dedication

In memory of my late dad, Hendrick Nkadimeng. In Thanksgiving to Holy Rosary Catholic Church and the Casa Italiana Community in Washington, DC.

I dedicate this to three dear friends, Kathleen Dunn, Dante Figueroa, and Francesco Isgrò, without whose help this work would not have been possible.

"God crowns the gifts of the grace that He has freely given" – St. Augustine (coronando merita nostra, Deus coronat dona sua)

Author's Note

This book highlights the importance of the theme of fraternity, especially at a time when fostering authentic relationships between the Global South and the Global North is so urgently needed. I therefore encourage a broader, well-thought-out understanding of fraternity as articulated by Pope Benedict XVI. This understanding is further developed in papal teachings such as those of Pope Francis and Pope Leo XIV. I pray that this work will serve as a valuable resource for readers working at the intersections of theology, social justice, human dignity, and the promotion of Catholic Social Teaching. At the same time, I hope it will help bridge the gap between the North and South, so we can find an effective model for sharing resources. *Caritas in Veritate* and *Africae Munus* remain highly relevant today as we face current global and local challenges.

Foreword

FATHER THABANG NKADIMENG was still Brother Thabang, a delegate from South Africa, when he and I attended the 2009 Second Special Assembly for Africa of the Synod of Bishops. This seems rather fitting for this book he has written on authentic fraternity in light of the writings of Pope Benedict XVI, who presided over that momentous worldwide gathering.

Fraternity is a familiar reality to the Church, each of us made brothers and sisters in Christ. Our fraternal nature and calling are foundational to Catholic Social Teaching as well, and they were the subject of an entire encyclical on the topic by Pope Francis, *Fratelli Tutti*, which built upon the past papal social magisterium and sought to contribute to the rebirth of a universal aspiration of fraternity. Yet, although peoples across the world have acknowledged we "should act towards one another in a spirit of brotherhood" (United Nations Universal Declaration of Human Rights), it is far from a reality today, nor is there agreement about what it even means.

Joseph Ratzinger's outstanding contributions to Catholic thought, both before and after he became pope, are undisputed. With the Lord having called him home, Father Thabang presents here his own valuable contribution with this study looking back at the influential legacy of this brilliant theologian on the question of fraternity.

Like his successor, Pope Benedict spoke and wrote often about fraternal solidarity. *Caritas in Veritate*, which is cited extensively in Fratelli Tutti, discusses the imperative of recognizing we are all one human family in the context of human development. Meanwhile, his post-synodal apostolic exhortation *Africae Munus* presents the Good News of fraternity as the way forward for the African people.

While there has been a space of years since these magisterial documents, I agree with Father Thabang that both are still relevant today and worthy of re-examination. *Caritas in Veritate* and *Africae Munus* continue to offer light for not only the African Church and people, but for the entire universal Church and all humanity, like the 2009 Synod itself, which far from being an isolated past event was but one component of the Church's ongoing synodality.

With all of Joseph Ratzinger's theology being so devoted to truth, a key word in both of these works naturally is "authentic" – authentic development, authentic humanism, and the establishment of authentic fraternity in comparison to the incomplete secular understanding. This distinction, which Father Thabang explores, has enormous implications for individual persons and society as a whole.

The sons and daughters of Africa who participated in the Synod enriched the gathering with their lived experiences. After listening to them, all of us who participated in that global discussion on the great African Continent – with its richness of spiritual traditions and sacred heritage extending back to Christian antiquity, its historical and contemporary struggles, and our human interconnectedness – brought home with us treasured memories. Then-Brother Thabang, however, from his perch as assistant to the General Secretariat, was in an especially privileged position to observe and come away with a keen knowledge and understanding of the mind and heart of the Holy Father Pope Benedict.

Being a son of the African diaspora, it was of great interest for me to learn of the pastoral concerns of the people and Church in Africa. At the same time, I told the Synod participants, in my experience as an American bishop, I knew of the remarkable gifts that Africa has bestowed on the United States and, indeed, on all the world. Thus, I can fully attest to Father Thabang's statement that "the greatest gift that Africa can give is faith."

The African clergy and religious who serve generously to the ends of the earth, as well as the wonderful immigrants from Africa who bring their deep faith with them, all challenge us in the West to rediscover our own spiritual traditions. In fact, Father Thabang would himself later become one of those missionaries from Africa to this mission territory that is the United States, and I was delighted when, in the providence of God, he arrived to be a priest in the Church of Washington where I am archbishop.

With this book, our brother Father Thabang continues to be a missionary, thereby offering a living example of his observation of Pope Benedict's hope "that Africa should live authentic fraternity and, as a result, should constitute an example to the whole world." Father Thabang as missionary is also apt with his adoption of Pope Benedict's recognition that authentic fraternity cannot be understood apart from Christology and the accompanying principles of love and truth, so that "the greatest service to development is a Christian humanism."

Make no mistake, Africa faces current challenges and has a terrible past of exploitation, colonialism, and violence, which we discussed at the 2009 Synod. The continent is thus often spoken of as being in need of development and progress, which in turn are often thought of in terms of technology, material goods, and economy. But true development, Father Thabang points out, is integral and considers the whole person, including the spiritual and transcendent dimension. In this respect, he notes that Pope Benedict saw Africa as a continent of hope due to her people's reception of the Christian faith. Consequently, in many important ways, Africa is more developed than many Western nations.

Here we come to the heart of the matter. Comparing historical ideas of fraternity, Father Thabang notes that Christianity "changed the whole notion of fraternity from being a mere notion of blood relations or a brotherhood of compatriots, to being a fraternity of all." Again and again, he hammers home that authentic fraternity – proclaimed as Good News by Christianity and necessary for real fruitful human development – is a communion of people joined by the values and vocation of love and truth, which accepts and cares for one another precisely as brothers and sisters in the family of God, and not merely as individuals and neighbors living side by side.

In our time, we see all around us a breakdown in social bonds and respect for the dignity of every human life. It is also painfully clear that the myriad of issues we are facing stems from not caring for our neighbor. Seeing these things happening all around us locally, nationally, and internationally, with a heavy cost to people's well-being, we know that we must speak out and work for justice, human dignity and authentic human development.

With his journey through Pope Benedict's notion of fraternity, which was echoed by Pope Francis in Fratelli Tutti, Father Thabang reminds us of the hope that has been offered us and proclaimed by the Church through the ages. It is the hope – which he adds is the goal of this book – "that the whole world will live as brothers and sisters working towards development guided by the principles of charity and truth." Much still needs to be done in realizing this authentic fraternity, but it is the only way out of the darkness and toward humanity becoming what we are meant to be.

Wilton Cardinal Gregory
Archbishop Emeritus of Washington

INTRODUCTION

The purpose of this book, entitled "AUTHENTIC FRATERNITY: The Notion of *Fraternitas* in Pope Benedict XVI's *Caritas in Veritate* and *Africae Munus*," is to present an analysis of the notion of fraternity as developed by Benedict XVI in his encyclical, and then to explore the relevance of this concept to Africa through a consideration of the Apostolic Exhortation, *Africae Munus*. By developing the theme of fraternity in relation to current social realities, *Caritas in Veritate* is related to the context of today's economic and social realities. The encyclical although published during the aftermath of the economic and financial crisis of 2008, is still relevant today.

In writing *Caritas in Veritate*, while taking the whole corpus of papal social teaching into account, Pope Benedict linked his concerns primarily to those expressed by Pope Paul VI's encyclical *Populorum Progressio* and responded to current social realities related to human development in a way similar to that which Paul VI used to exhort the international society to work for development.

While the encyclical belongs in the corpus of the Church's social teaching, its full understanding requires a consideration of the whole of Pope Benedict's substantive *corpus theologicum*. While it is his magisterial teaching which is the primary concern of the thesis, attention is also paid to his writings as a theologian, under the name of Joseph Ratzinger. Due attention is therefore given to how the notion of *Fraternitas* is affected by the Pope's (and in a secondary way Ratzinger's) positions on Christology, ecclesiology, Sacramentology, anthropology, eschatology, pastoral theology and political theologies. Since the encyclical is addressed to all peoples, whatever their religious faith, it incorporates these themes in a way that they may rightly belong within such an address.

There is a difference between how these themes occur in the encyclical and how they are incorporated into *Africae Munus* which is addressed to the Catholic community of the continent. When he has offered an analysis of the current state of development in the encyclical, inclusive of social and economic realities and in light of his understanding of the human, Pope Benedict introduces the notion of fraternity as a key to the position which he wishes to offer to the world community's consideration. His point of departure is Christological, but he wishes to present Christ in a way that is suited to the large population which he has in mind. He begins his encyclical with these words: "Charity in truth, to which Jesus Christ bore witness by his earthly life and especially by his death and resurrection, is the principal driving force behind the authentic development of every person and of all humanity."[1] Here it is clear that he presents Christ as witness to truth and charity, a point which all may appreciate even if they do not subscribe to Christian dogma.

The role of the Church, as evident in *Caritas in Veritate*, and as will be outlined in this book, is of paramount importance to the development of the human person in its own witness to truth and charity. The Pope has both material and spiritual poverty in mind, as is even clearer in the Post-Synodal Exhortation, *Africae Munus*. Benedict is convinced that poverty cannot be eradicated only by states and other temporal powers but needs people and community which testify to the spiritual dimension of human reality. Obviously, Benedict gives primacy to the Church's role in this regard, but he also recognizes that it works alongside other communities and persons who are likewise attentive to the spiritual and to the transcendent.

---

[1] *Caritas in Veritate*, 1.

On the other hand, in the letter to the African churches, Benedict gives primary attention to the role of the Church while addressing African concerns of human, social, and political realities, which are pertinent to non-African countries also experiencing material or spiritual underdevelopment.

The first chapter of this book deals with the purpose and method of *Caritas in Veritate,* in which the encyclical will be placed in its proper context. The principles of *caritas* and *veritas* lead to the proper understanding of the theme of *Fraternitas* – the building of a society where people accept one another as brothers and sisters and not merely neighbors living side by side. In this chapter, it is made clear to what realities the Pope wants to attend and how he reflects on both the material and spiritual factors at stake in human development.

The second chapter deals directly with the theme of *fraternitas* – the core of this book. It is in this chapter that fraternity will not be taken in isolation but placed in conjunction with its related terms such as *communio, solidarietas, subsidiaritas, societas,* and the phenomenon of globalization. By understanding this notion of fraternity concretely and not just conceptually, we can then understand the driving force behind Benedict's *Caritas in Veritate.*[2]

The third chapter continues the themes in the preceding two chapters, exploring the implications of *fraternitas* for full human development. The point of departure is to view development as a vocation, as taught by both Paul VI and Benedict XVI respectively.

The fourth chapter moves from *Caritas in Veritate* to *Africae Munus* in which the theme of *fraternitas* finds a prominent place. Although directed to the Church in Africa, *Africae Munus* relates to *Caritas in Veritate* in applying the under-

---

[2] *Caritas in Veritate,* 1.

standing of its theme to the work of reconciliation, justice and peace. The African stories of fraternity offer a narrative and pastoral dimension on how the Church is involved in the social and political sphere. It is in Christ, therefore, that a new brotherhood of love and truth is created for the integral development of humanity.

In conclusion, chapter five evaluates critical comments on *Caritas in Veritate*. It is in this chapter too that pastoral ways of overcoming the difficulty of the encyclical's text are presented. It is this book's goal to offer a thorough understanding of the notion of *fraternitas* present in Pope Benedict XVI's *Caritas in Veritate* and *Africae Munus,* with the hope that the whole world will live as brothers and sister working towards development guided by the principles of charity and truth.

Chapter One

The Purpose and Method of *Caritas in Veritate*

THE PURPOSE OF *CARITAS IN VERITATE*

In the first pages of his *Introduction to Christianity*, then-cardinal Joseph Ratzinger employed Søren Kierkegaard's famous tale of a clown's futile mission to warn a village threatened by fire, in order to illustrate how the theologian's vocation to a world closed in on itself and beset by unbelief compares strikingly to that of the clown in Kierkegaard's story.

> [A] travelling circus in Denmark caught fire. The manager thereupon sent the clown, who was already dressed and made up for the performance, into the neighboring village to fetch help, especially as there was a danger that the fire would spread across the fields of dry stubble and engulf the village itself. The clown hurried into the village and requested the inhabitants to come as quickly as possible to the blazing circus and help to put the fire out. But the villagers took the clown's shouts simply for an excellent piece of advertising, meant to attract as many people as possible to the performance; they applauded the clown and laughed till they cried. The clown felt more like weeping than laughing; he tried in vain to get people to be serious, to make it clear to them that this was no stunt, that he was not pretending but was in bitter earnest, that there really was a fire. His supplications only increased the laughter; people thought he was playing his part splendidly – until finally the fire did engulf the village; it was too late for help, and both circus and village were burned to the ground.[3]

---

[3] Joseph Ratzinger, *Introduction to Christianity* (San Francisco: Ignatius Press, 2004), 39-40.

The analogy applies with equal pertinence to Pope Benedict XVI's message of human development in *Caritas in Veritate*, which he delivered to a world that fails to heed the urgent call to construct fraternal bonds of development, mutual understanding, and transparency.

Even though the social teachings of the Church are meant to recall society to its duty of working towards mutual development in a way that is integrally human – which is to say, in charity and truth – this message has seldom been taken seriously by society, precisely in as much as social reforms require challenging human behaviors that are harmful to others, and creating ways that contribute to the development of all. It would appear disciplines such as economics – like the villagers in Kierkegaard's allegory – are not open to the warning of the Church, considering themselves to be sciences independent of, and unrelated to the queen of the sciences: theology.[4]

Benedict XVI is hardly the first pontiff to pen an encyclical on social teaching. It is, rather, to Pope Leo XIII's 1891 encyclical *Rerum novarum*, that historians commonly attribute the honor of constituting a visible starting point of properly so-called social doctrine theory. For his part, Pope Benedict XVI has identified Pope Paul VI's encyclical of 1967 *Populorum Progressio*, as representing the "*Rerum novarum* of our times". In *Caritas in Veritate*, Benedict XVI considers both his predecessors' encyclicals highly relevant in the development of a continuous thread of social doctrine responding both to the perennial social problems, yet to be resolved, as well as to social problems manifesting in contemporary society.

Many countries had to confront an economic and financial crisis before the publication of *Caritas in Veritate* which, were the social teachings of the Church to have been

---

[4] Cf. *Caritas in Veritate*, 34.

heeded, particularly in *Populorum Progressio*, it would have helped avert the conflagration of this crisis and many other concomitant social problems which the world today finds itself facing. Despite this failure, the economic crisis and the crisis of faith in today's world, nevertheless, opens a new path to confronting the challenge of evaluating economic and social systems that have not proved successful – a path characterized by the notion of fraternity.

It is through fraternity that social injustices which occur in the world would better be eradicated since fraternity recalls people to their vocation of being brothers and sisters and not mere individuals and neighbors. "As society becomes ever more globalized, it makes us neighbors but does not make us brothers."[5]

In *Caritas in Veritate* Benedict XVI continues in the tradition of his predecessors, Leo XIII, Paul VI, and John Paul II, becoming, himself, a moral voice in the world today: addressing his encyclical to "all people of good will." He becomes a figure recalling society to Divine Law, to natural law and to the fundamental dignity inherent to every human person. *Caritas in Veritate*'s very first paragraph observes that charity and truth are intrinsic to man, but need to be discovered; and that Christ is the revelation in which people discover their true humanity (1). In concluding his encyclical, Benedict XVI returns to this notion for an integral humanism found in Christ, by emphasizing that, "[W]ithout God man neither knows which way to go, nor even understands who he is...The greatest service to development, then, is a Christian humanism."[6]

A Christian humanism goes against the definition of humanism as simply a human philosophy of life that can be held without necessarily believing in God. Christian

---

[5] *Caritas in Veritate*, 19.
[6] Ibid., 78. "*Sine Deo nescit homo quo se vertat neque intellegere potest quis ipse sit... Ad progressionem iuvandam maxima ideo est vis christianus humanismus...*"

humanism then will not condone a humanism that is atheistic or agnostic but proposes a humanism that finds its origin in God, and that the moral codes to live in this world come from God. "The fool says in his heart, 'there is no God'."[7]

Although *Caritas in Veritate* is a social encyclical addressed to all people of good will, it is also a teaching of faith addressed to the faithful. The challenges posed by Benedict are addressed not only to the political world entrusted with the prerogative of serving citizens of the world, but challenge the community of faith to live the Christian values, especially truth. "A Christianity of charity without truth would be more or less interchangeable with a pool of good sentiments, helpful for social cohesion, but of little relevance. In other words, there would no longer be any real place for God in the world."[8]

The encyclical cannot be seen, therefore, solely as a social document but as an ecclesiological encyclical, calling us to communion – the manifestation of the reality of the Church, present in the modern world.[9] The Christian community has its role to play in the social and political world, and this role finds its source in Christ who transforms the human being into a self-conscious person: living and putting into practice the Gospel values in all spectrums of life, whether in family life, in the work place, in politics or wherever he finds himself. It is a cosmic role that is guided by the need to work for justice and peace and the integrity of creation.

By this encyclical, and particularly by speaking of fraternity and Christian humanism, Jacques Maritain's plea, voiced in the 1930s is worth mentioning.

---

[7] Psalm 14:1.
[8] *Caritas in Veritate*, 4.
[9] Cf. *Gaudium et Spes*.

It is high time for Christians to bring things back to truth, reintegrating in the fullness of their original source those hopes for justice and those nostalgias for the communion on which the world's sorrow feeds and which are themselves misdirected, thus awaking a cultural and temporal force of Christian inspiration able to act on history and to be a support to men...It is not to the dynamism or imperialism of race or class or nation that this humanism asks men to sacrifice themselves; it is to a better life for their brothers and to the concrete good of the community of human persons; it is to the humble truth of brotherly love to be realized – at the cost of an always difficult effort and of a relative poverty – in the social order and the structures of common life. In this way such a humanism can make man grow in communion, and if so, it cannot be less than a heroic humanism.[10]

CARITAS IN THE ENCYCLICAL

Charity in truth means to abide in the truth charitably; being in dialogue with those who have not yet discovered the meaning of truth, of charity, of fraternity, or even the value of human life as it is from conception to natural death. It is Christ who constitutes "Truth," and transforms particular truths to correspond to his dual command: love of God and love of neighbor.

It is Christ, then, who reveals to man his inner self and his vocation. The driving force of *Caritas in Veritate* is "charity in truth, to which Jesus Christ bore witness by his earthly life and especially by his death and resurrection."[11] It is the sacrament of baptism that incorporates everyone into the death and resurrection of Jesus. By accepting baptism, the believer dies to self so that he may rise with Christ - embracing the "I" of Christ, to which with St. Paul the Apostle, he may rise to say: "It is no longer I who live but Christ who

---

[10] J. Maritain, *Integral Humanism* (New York: Charles Scribner's Sons, 1968), 6-7.
[11] *Caritas in Veritate*, 1.

lives in me"[12]. By rising with Christ, man discovers the inherent gifts of charity and truth, "planted by God in the heart and mind of every human person."[13]

What is *caritas* and *veritas*, then, that is planted by God in the heart and mind of every human person? The answer is found in the *fons et origo* of each one's vocation, namely God. Benedict XVI defines *caritas* as "an extraordinary force which leads people to opt for courageous and generous engagement in the field of justice and peace. It is a force that has its origin in God, Eternal Love and Absolute Truth" (1).[14] It has been reduced to the subjective sensation of each individual. Such a notion of love fuels relativism, which has gravely undermined the notion of fraternity, since by it each individual seeks his own good, in his own way and by whatever means. Love ceases to be understood any more as mutual self-donation, as oblative love, according to the model of God becoming man in order to demonstrate the depth of his predilection for humanity. God being love (*Deus caritas est*), therefore, confirms the fact that any humanism which would deny Christ could not constitute true humanism, since it lacks the very foundation of authentic love.

Opting for a Christian humanism is to remove the ambiguities present in the definition of "humanism," it is to affirm God as the center of man and not man as the center of his own existence; here is where Christian humanism opposes Anthropocentric humanism. This is why Benedict speaks not only of humanism but of Christian humanism. Jacques Maritain, in his *Integral Humanism*, attests that Christian humanism "recognizes that God is the center of

---

[12] Gal 2:20.
[13] *Caritas in Veritate*, 1.
[14] Amor – «caritas» – *magna est vis quae personas impellit ut animose studioseque in iustitiae ac pacis provincia agant. Est quidem vis, quae a Deo principium sumit, Amore sane aeterno absolutaque Veritate.*

man; it implies the Christian conception of man, sinner and redeemed, and the Christian conception of grace and freedom..."[15]

In the same way that baptism sets us free from darkness and sin, so does the discovery of truth. As John the Beloved disciple intimates, "The truth will set you free."[16] However, being a Person, Christ, Himself finds man, not man the truth. Yet rationalism somehow exalted man to a state of thinking of himself as the center of his own life, hence Descartes' affirmation *Cogito, ergo sum* (I think, therefore I am) rather than *Cogitor, ergo sum* (I am thought of, therefore I am).

Without truth, man lives as slave to falsity, chained by what is not the truth, remains imprisoned within himself and can never reach that integral human development which is his right to discover and nurture. Setting man free through the discovery of the intrinsic gift of truth, God liberates him also to develop himself through adherence to God's plan for him. "[I]n this plan, he finds his truth, and through adherence to this truth he becomes free."[17]

Caritas in Veritate, which was published during a time of economic and financial crisis in many countries, demonstrates how opting for the truth constructs the bridge linking ancient social concerns with those of the modern world.

> The great challenge before us, accentuated by the problems of development in this global era and made even more urgent by the economic and financial crisis, is to demonstrate, in thinking and behavior, not only that traditional principles of social ethics like transparency, honesty and responsibility cannot be ignored or attenuated, but also that in *commercial relationships* the *principle of*

---

[15] Jacques Maritain, *Integral Humanism* (New York: Charles Scribner's Sons, 1968), 27-28.
[16] John 8:22.
[17] *Caritas in Veritate*, 1.

gratuitousness and the logic of gift as an expression of fraternity can and must *find their place within normal economic activity*.[18] (36)

According to Pope Benedict XVI, the problems of development, human, social, and economic, can be solved only by a return to the traditional principles of social ethics, such as transparency (*integritas*), honesty and responsibility, and particularly by the principle of gratuitousness, and the logic of gift as an expression of fraternity. The logic of gift as an expression of fraternity is linked to these principles because it is only through fraternity that people or nations can share natural resources. The pursuit for development has to be guided by the values of charity and truth.

The absence of the traditional principles as pointed by Pope Benedict is not Christian but is typical of an anthropocentric humanism, seeking its *telos* within itself rather than in eternal life. The exaltation of an anthropocentric humanism is unfortunately the tragedy of modern culture, visible in economics, technology, and the like. This kind of humanism leaves God as an 'idea' or in Nietzschean terms 'dead'.[19] It remains an open question as to whether Pope Benedict reaffirmed that the world should embrace Christianity in order to have a true humanism. However, he does open dialogue between faith and practice, faith and cultures, faith and reason, and finally faith and all working in economics, politics and human development (78).

---

[18] *Summa provocatio quae nobis ante oculos versatur, emersa e quaestionibus circa progressionem, hoc globalizationis tempore, et urgentior in dies ob crisim oeconomicam-nummariam, in eo est ut demonstret tam cogitationibus quam moribus, quod non solum tradita principia ethicae socialis, qualia sunt* **integritas**, *honestas et responsalitas, neque neglegi neque mitigari possunt, verum etiam quod in relationibus mercatoriis principium gratuitatis et logica doni uti manifestatio fraternitatis possunt et debent locum invenire intra consuetam actionem oeconomicam.* (My emphasis. The word *integritas*, is translated in the English as transparency rather than integrity).

[19] *Caritas in Veritate*, 78.

Where there is no fraternity, there will be no honesty, neither transparency nor responsibility. Where fraternity is lacking, human beings cease to be treated as subjects but are viewed reductively, as objects, capable of easy manipulation. The failure of putting into practice the notion of fraternity can be ascribed to a selfish understanding of development, where a fair and honest exchange of gifts is not observed. True fraternity means to seek my good and the good of others; however, my good should not infringe on the good and freedom of others, that is to say, my pursuit for good should not deprive others of their natural goods such as freedom, including their right to private property.

Globalization has contributed the benefit of social networks between people from all spectrums of life. In many instances, however, people communicate merely as neighbors, one to another, not as brothers and sisters. Social media may be understood as instances where "friendships" are created (on-line or otherwise) which remain but on a superficial (or even immoral) level. Charity-in-truth challenges these kinds of problems, experienced mostly by the youth. From this perspective, *Caritas in Veritate,* while addressed to people of all ages, challenges the youth, who are the proper people to address the present and future in charity and truth, particularly in the area of technology.

"Without truth, without trust and love for what is true, there is no social conscience and responsibility, and social action ends up serving private interests and the logic of power, resulting in social fragmentation, especially in a globalized society at difficult times like the present."[20] Just as there is, through modern means of communication, a technological network between people, so too, a network of love needs to be fostered in order to engage fraternally and

---

[20] *Caritas in Veritate,* 5.

collaborate in the design of God the Father for the integral development of all peoples (21).

Globalization will result in authentic development only where it builds communion between persons. Globalization ought, therefore, to imitate the communion that exists in the Trinity. This is the communion that is innately present in family life, that which is realized at the Eucharistic celebration, and which concretizes Jesus' prayer of unity: *'ut unum sint.'*[21] Globalization needs to overcome the challenge of elevating the individual over the person; the person is called to be in relation with others, whereas individuality emphasizes the independence of the singular.

Pope Benedict XVI's encyclicals, *Deus caritas est* and *Spe salvi*, illustrate what lies at the pope's heart, that is: love of God and love of the human person. Towards the end of *Caritas in Veritate*, humanity is exhorted to acknowledge God. Only by so doing can humanity truly be called human. "*A humanism which excludes God is an inhuman humanism.* Only a humanism open to the Absolute can guide us in the promotion and building of forms of social and civic life – structures, institutions, culture and *ethos* – without exposing us to the risk of becoming ensnared by the fashions of the moment."[22]

Benedict's call for an international authority to guide globalized society may be seen as a call to prioritize the dignity of the human person, combating, *inter alia*, poverty, greed, war, terrorism, the denial of the right to religious freedom, and replacing them with human values that lead to the development of the human person, of the family and of society at large. An international authority must not, however, exclude God. It is the prerogative of Christianity

---

[21] John 17:22.
[22] *Caritas in Veritate*, 78.

to reclaim its rightful place of evangelization in the world, as is the Divine Commission.

Integral human development can come about only through Christ. Rejection of Christ implies a return to the pre-Christian world, which is impossible since the Word has definitively 'become flesh'. The purpose of *Caritas in Veritate*, then, is to remind society of the true meaning of charity and truth – and to remind society of the purpose of the incarnation could be said to constitute the guiding theology to this encyclical, wherein Christ is shown to be the perfect man who reveals what humanity truly is. To return to Kierkegaard's story, then: the world can indeed be freed from the fire of injustices, not by a clown, but by truly Christian humanity whose voice is forever credible.

CARITAS IN VERITATE IN RELATION TO POPULORUM PROGRESSIO

Caritas in Veritate commemorates over forty years of the publication of *Populorum Progressio* of Pope Paul VI on integral human development. Pope John Paul II celebrated the twentieth anniversary of *Populorum Progressio* in 1987 by the publication of the encyclical *Sollicitudo rei socialis*. Drew Christiansen SJ in his article entitled "Metaphysics and Society: A Commentary on *Caritas in Veritate*", states that "[S]ome thought a new social encyclical would appear in 2007 on the 40th anniversary of Pope Paul VI's *Populorum Progressio*, but it did not. Then came the financial crisis of 2008, and many observers wondered what the Vatican had to say about the most serious economic crisis since the Great Depression."[23]

It was not until the 29th of June 2009 that *Caritas in Veritate* was published in which Benedict XVI continued Paul

---

[23] Drew Christiansen, *Metaphysics and Society: A Commentary on Caritas in Veritate* (Theological Studies, June 2010; 71, 2), 3-4.

VI's and John Paul II's line of thought in the Church's *corpus* of social teaching. The immediate link that one notices between the encyclicals is the Christology inherent within the theme of development. Paul VI affirms that "life in Christ is the first and principal factor of development,"[24] a notion underlined by Benedict in *Caritas in Veritate* no. 8.

Benedict has a thought-provoking way in which he addresses the social issues. Ecclesiology is never divorced from the social doctrine of the Church and he even states that *Populorum Progressio* would be a document without roots if it were seen apart from the "Tradition of the apostolic faith"[25]. The Second Vatican Council is linked in a close way to *Populorum Progressio* as Paul VI states in the opening pages of the encyclical and as later John Paul II recounts.[26] Consequently, for Benedict these encyclicals are not only social awareness documents but are also documents of faith, linked to the whole life of the Church. The link that these encyclicals have with the whole life of the Church was well expressed by Paul VI in saying: "The whole Church, in all her being and acting – when she proclaims, when she celebrates, when she performs works of charity – is engaged in promoting integral human development."[27]

The need for a Christian humanism is therefore a point of departure, defining what man is and what kind of humanism he should strive to achieve. This need for a proper Christian humanism was also necessary for the saints. St. Eugene de Mazenod – the bishop of Marseilles and founder of the Missionary Oblates of Mary Immaculate, for example, exhorted his missionaries to help people firstly to be

---

[24] *Populorum Progressio*, 16.
[25] Cf. *Caritas in Veritate*, 10.
[26] Cf. *Populorum Progressio*, 3-5.
[27] *Populorum Progressio*, 14; *Caritas in Veritate* , 11.

human, then Christian, and finally help them to become saints.[28]

Charity is the greatest of all the theological virtues because it transforms the earthly city and prepares for the eternal city. Faith and hope are important in the earthly city, but only charity remains in the eternal city. Therefore, to love is to be looking forward to the beatific vision in which love will gaze at love *par excellence*. If in the earthly city man may be transformed by charity, then he is in an experience of the 'already and not yet,' where he is transformed in the earthly city and given a taste of the Heavenly Jerusalem.[29]

The issues of people living in great poverty and misery mentioned by Paul VI, particularly in countries still living under colonialism or those who were about to gain their independence in the wake of 1967 has not changed according to Benedict XVI (33). Although colonialism was nefarious and nations needed to be independent what followed after independence in some places is worse or pretty much the same kind of torment caused by fellow leaders to their countrymen. The relationship, therefore, of *Populorum Progressio* and *Caritas in Veritate* on integral human development should be seen within the framework of striving for a truly Christian humanism embedded in Christology, Ecclesiology and Social concern and guiding towards the Heavenly Jerusalem, the Eternal City.

FUNDAMENTAL PRINCIPLES OF CHARITY AND TRUTH

Charity and truth are fundamental principles to an integral human development. Without charity and without truth, humanity in all its aspects runs the risk of underdevelopment. Underdevelopment is primarily due to a lack of fraternity, where sharing is not a value but a mentality of "I

---

[28] Preface to Constitutions and Rules (Rome: Oblates of Mary Immaculate, 2000), 22.
[29] Cf. *Caritas in Veritate*, 7.

give you this, and you give me that" prevails; this mentality has, in many cases, even taken away the natural rights of people, especially the natural gift of freedom.

Where there is no fraternity, neither charity nor truth can exist for the development of society. Pope Benedict states that "Underdevelopment has an even more important cause than lack of deep thought: it is 'the lack of brotherhood among individuals and peoples."[30] For example, the three pillars that characterize France are: *Liberté, égalité, fraternité*. It is striking to see that fraternity is one of the pillars that characterize France; however, it remains debatable whether this pillar is properly practiced as a brotherhood among individuals and peoples, not just among the French.

The notion of fraternity is primarily of blood relations but has been transformed by Christ, in which all Christians are brothers to one another. However, the French Revolution and the eighteenth-century Enlightenment based fraternity as a result of this world – from the fatherland – and not from the Paternity of God. France as a country, for example, has a Platonic understanding of fraternity where one's fellow citizen is a brother. However, as was understood by Plato, someone from outside the community will not be regarded a brother, but a *barbaros*.[31]

Human solidarity is presented under the complementary aspects of social principle and moral virtue.[32] Society is at the service of the human person; therefore, the human person as a member of society is to be served in view of the common good. There is no contradiction, however, between the person and society because the human person lives in society. It is constitutive of man to be in relation. "Sometimes modern man is wrongly convinced that he is the sole

---

[30] *Caritas in Veritate*, 19.
[31] *Menexenos*, 239 a.
[32] Cf. Solidarity is first and foremost a sense of responsibility on the part of everyone with regard to everyone. *Caritas in Veritate*, 38.

author of himself, his life and society. This is a presumption that follows from being selfishly closed in upon himself..."[33] Solidarity is a social principle because "no man is an island"' [citation needed], and it is a moral virtue because to live together means making sure that everyone lives well.

Calling for cooperation at an international level as well as the local level is a call to create a humanism which disregards national borders but brings people together under one cosmos as brothers and sisters. This cooperation is between humans who together strive to build a just world. It is based on fraternal values where the suffering people are alleviated from their suffering. "*Feed the hungry* is an ethical imperative for the universal Church, as she responds to the teachings of her Founder, the Lord Jesus, concerning solidarity and the sharing of goods" (27).

Christians are encouraged not to be attached to private property but to share everything, as did the first Christian community. The sharing of goods then, in the light of the Gospel, becomes a necessary condition for an authentic *sequela Christi*. Having everything in common is to enter in relationship with Jesus the Teacher, and with one another. It is living as brothers and sisters to one another.

On the other hand, at an international level it is important to ask the question, "What are global common goods?" The global common goods, properly understood, are those that due to their nature cannot be sold nor bought. These goods are, by their nature, necessary to the human person. These goods could be justice or freedom, and the like. They are intrinsic necessities to the human person and contribute to his development and ability to enhance the development of the society.

In *Populorum Progressio*, Paul VI seeks a human development that is based on justice, not only for certain people but

---

[33] *Caritas in Veritate*, 34.

for all people. By raising social questions, Paul VI has the intention of speaking for the voiceless who suffer poverty, illiteracy, slavery and wars.

> From the economic point of view, this meant their active participation, on equal terms, in the international economic process; from the social point of view, it meant their evolution into educated societies marked by solidarity; from the political point of view, it meant the consolidation of democratic regimes capable of ensuring freedom and peace.[34]

Globalization (the explosion of worldwide interdependence),[35] according to Benedict XVI, was partially foreseen by Paul VI; although it was not evident how rapidly it would advance (33). Globalization, as a positive phenomenon can strengthen the process of unity among peoples and nations and create the 'fraternity' that should be sought by all. However, this phenomenon could give rise to unemployment in many countries, it could cause harm to the environment and could also increase the gap between the rich and the poor where 'the strong subdue the weak' (36).

Benedict XVI states that the principle of subsidiarity "is first and foremost a form of assistance to the human person via the autonomy of intermediate bodies" (57). Pope Pius XI was the first to speak of the principle of subsidiarity in his encyclical of 1931 *Quadragesimo anno*. Pius XI was aware of a superior/inferior problem between states; He was adamant to uphold respect for the human person and indicate the need that man has for society.[36] Both pontiffs would advocate for a reciprocal link between subsidiarity and solidarity.

---

[34] *Caritas in Veritate*, 21.
[35] See *Caritas in Veritate*, 6, 7, 9, 23, 25, 27, 37, 39, 41, 46, 47, 50, 55, 58, 59, 69, 70, 73.
[36] *Quadragesimo Anno*, 86.

"The state is not the totality."[37] The state is composed of individuals, and it is always at the service of the human person. The tension between Church and state can prove to be tricky, especially where it is not clear when and how the Church should intervene in the public sphere of politics. Nevertheless, the fundamental principles of charity and truth are always to be upheld, be it by the Church or by the state. Upholding these principles contributes to an integral human development and is the responsibility of all peoples, not only of macro-bodies (social, economic and political), but also of micro-relationships (friends and family).[38]

THE HUMAN COMMUNITY AS A FRATERNAL COMMUNITY

"The human community that we build by ourselves can never, purely by its own strength, be a fully fraternal community, nor can it overcome every division and become a truly universal community" (34). This strong statement from Pope Benedict seems to say that it is only through the fundamental principles of charity and truth that real development can take place; these principles coming forth as gifts of God given gratuitously. However, Benedict XVI seems to also affirm that it is only through acknowledging God as "Our Father", that true development can take place, because then as brothers and sisters we would be creating a human family built on charity and truth; it is having God as the Father and foundation of the universal community.

The Church needs to "proclaim" the Truth (Christ) and needs to remind the state of the value of the truth. Where norms are absent in a state, it is the Church that needs to take a bold step of reminding people of the need to return to the norms. The Church, therefore, never claims the truth but proclaims without faltering. "[T]estimony *to Christ's*

---

[37] Joseph Ratzinger, *Church, Ecumenism, and Politics*, (San Francisco, Ignatius Press: 2008), 145.
[38] *Caritas in Veritate*, 2.

charity, through works of justice, peace and development, is part and parcel of evangelization, because Jesus Christ, who loves us, is concerned with the whole person"(15).[39]

In a pluralistic society it becomes difficult to listen to one moral voice, but only the voice of the Truth can be listened to. Christ is that Word and that Truth, and the moral voice is like the voice of St. John the Baptist crying out in the wilderness.[40] The Church, analogically, is like St. John the Baptist crying out in the wilderness for an embrace of the Christian values of charity and truth in order to be a true fraternal community.

On a Catholic pastoral level, the Truth can be proclaimed only by very well catechized Catholics. Today's generation is one that is intellectually inquisitive, and this should be taken as an opportunity to not only teach basic Christian principles but to also teach the concepts and how to practice the faith. People should be taught how to pray with devotion - a prayer like the Rosary. They should also be taught about more complex issues such as divine law, natural law, Church-state relations etc. The Rite of Christian Initiation for Adults ("RCIA") catechesis needs to be re-visited in many ways and make it adaptable to a deeper theological catechesis.

In regard to the family of nations, Benedict advocates for a true world political authority. His words cannot go unmentioned:

> In the face of the unrelenting growth of global interdependence, there is a strongly felt need, even in the midst of a global recession, for a reform of the *United Nations Organization,* and likewise of *economic institutions and international finance,* so that the concept of the family of

---

[39] *Christi caritatis testificatio per iustitiae, pacis progressionisque opera pars quidem est evangelizationis, quandoquidem Iesu Christo, qui nos diligit, cordi est totus homo.*
[40] John 1:22-23.

nations can acquire real teeth. One also senses the urgent need to find innovative ways of implementing the principle of the *responsibility to protect* and of giving poorer nations an effective voice in shared decision-making. This seems necessary in order to arrive at a political, juridical and economic order which can increase and give direction to international cooperation for the development of all peoples in solidarity. To manage the global economy; to revive economies hit by the crisis; to avoid any deterioration of the present crisis and the greater imbalances that would result; to bring about integral and timely disarmament, food security and peace; to guarantee the protection of the environment and to regulate migration: for all this, there is urgent need of a true *world political authority*...[41]

The capital products today are much bigger than the sovereign nation, so Catholics need to rethink the nation-state. Big nations that are economically very powerful need to see themselves as brothers and not mere neighbors to poorer countries. For a proper global interdependence, it is imperative that all nations, countries, and states work together in a fraternal way and not in a dominating way. No country should suffer as a result of the decisions made by another.

Benedict's analysis of fraternity clearly comes from his understanding of what baptism effects in us, – we become children of God, members of his Holy Church and brother and sisters to one another. We become a family. Therefore, a fraternal community is one made up of brothers and sisters who together make one body.

The notion of fraternity however needs to be understood in the same light in which the Fatherhood of God is understood. God the Father is known in relation to his Son Jesus, and it is this relationship of love that is communicated

---

[41] *Caritas in Veritate*, 67.

to those who accept Christ and the Father. Hence, the adopted sons of God can also cry out "*Abba*." [cite Scripture]

Chapter Two

Fraternitas

AN ANALYSIS OF THE UNDERSTANDING OF *FRATERNITAS*

In *Caritas in Veritate,* Benedict XVI does not give a working definition of fraternity *per se,* but simply speaks of the principle of gratuitousness as an expression of fraternity, and the same notion is closely linked to reciprocity (34). In the same line of thought he also states that *Populorum Progressio* "repeatedly underlines the urgent need for reform" (20).[42]

The need for reform is a call to reflect on development and on what has led to underdevelopment; therefore, ways in which development has been sought but has not produced fruit, must be 'reformed.' It is clear, however, that the notion of fraternity stems from God who is love; and that when people perceive that they are loved by God, they are able, in turn, to extend this love to others. *"God's love calls us to move beyond the limited and the ephemeral, it gives us the courage to continue seeking and working for the benefit of all…"* (78: emphasis textual). Accordingly, charity is the foundation of authentic fraternity.[43]

The notion of fraternity is based on relationships, evidently; underlining the fact that 'no man is an island' and that reciprocal love is necessary in all spectrums of life. If there is to be any reform, therefore, it must produce truly fraternal bonds between people, which reforms human relations from individual to mega-relationships such as politics and economics. "Our lives are involved with one another; through innumerable interactions they are linked

---

[42] Cf. *Populorum Progressio,* 3, 29, 32.
[43] *Populorum Progressio* mentions the notion of fraternity/brotherhood a number of times in numbers: 44, 66, 71, 73, 75, 78, 82, 85, and 86.

together. No one lives alone. No one sins alone. No one is saved alone. The lives of others continually spill over into mine, in what I think, say, do and achieve. And, conversely, my life spills over into that of others, for better and for worse."[44]

Christian brotherhood should be considered from the perspective of salvation history, and within Christology in which God, who in Christ has made Himself the brother of all, becomes the model for all true Christian humanism. Although brotherhood finds its basis in the Paternity of God who creates man in his own image and likeness, it is only in Christ, through Whom man is redeemed from sin, which separates him from God, that man is once more reconciled with God as Father, and man regains his original and proper place of being son and brother to all. Thus, the redeemed regain their place in the Trinitarian communion. As *imago Dei*, man returns into the Trinitarian communion of the Father, the Son, and the Holy Spirit.

Brotherhood is properly speaking of blood relations. Historically, it has also been extended to compatriots whereby citizens of the same land would regard one another as brothers. It is a notion which, in many cultures, has also been extended to friendship. Therefore, relations of close family ties, of friendship and of citizenship, can constitute brotherhood; but, by implication, this also suggests that those who lack such relations fall outside the bonds of brotherhood and could not be regarded as brothers. In this sense, therefore brotherhood, strictly understood, knows boundaries.

The boundaries implicit in such an understanding of brotherhood give rise to intolerance and hatred, and which, in many places has provoked genocides, xenophobia and underdevelopment. The genocide in Rwanda, for example,

---

[44] *Spe Salvi*, 48.

was based on a tribal form of brotherhood where those who are outside "my tribe" are not "'my brothers" and therefore can be eliminated. The intrinsically evil system of apartheid in the Republic of South Africa was also founded on this false concept of brotherhood with boundaries.

Caritas in Veritate does not ignore the sort of fraternity which arises among family members, citizens and friends, but develops the notion of fraternity to extend to the whole cosmos.[45] The definition of fraternity in the light of *Caritas in Veritate* is based on the Paternity of God and is defined by Christ who as Son of God and brother of all, makes of his brothers, brothers to one another and this kind of brotherhood knows no boundaries.

CARITAS CHRISTI URGET NOS

At the origin of a fraternity inherently bounded by limitations lies a Marxist dialectic of competition. Although postulating in the use of the word "comrade," a notion apparently similar to brotherhood, Marxist solidarity is rooted in a socio-political relation rather than in the Paternity of God or even on a common fatherland. "Hence Marxism involves, from the beginning, a division of the world, intended by Marx as a purely social division; now – as a result of the Russian Revolution and of world politics – Marxism has become a political division into two opposing blocs of states…Brotherhood toward some involves enmity towards others."[46]

This form of brotherhood, in the Marxist understanding is driven by materialism and a disregard of the values inherent in man. In *Spe salvi* Benedict noted some of Marx's errors in embracing a 'materialistic goal' and disregarding the nature of man as such.

---

[45] Cf. *Caritas in Veritate*, 53.
[46] Joseph Ratzinger, *The Meaning of Christian Brotherhood* (San Francisco: Ignatius Press, 1993), 17.

Marx not only omitted to work out how this new world would be organized — which should, of course, have been unnecessary. His silence on this matter follows logically from his chosen approach. His error lay deeper. He forgot that man always remains man. He forgot man and he forgot man's freedom. He forgot that freedom always remains also freedom for evil. He thought that once the economy had been put right, everything would automatically be put right. His real error is materialism: man, in fact, is not merely the product of economic conditions, and it is not possible to redeem him purely from the outside by creating a favorable economic environment.[47]

Accordingly, the way of reform proposed by Pope Benedict (but initiated by Paul VI) concerns the establishment of authentic fraternity. Reform as has been understood implies reflecting on both 'form' and 'matter'. "It is Christ's charity that drives us on: *'caritas Christi urget nos'* (2 *Cor* 5:14). The urgency is inscribed not only in things, it is not derived solely from the rapid succession of events and problems, but also from the very matter that is at stake: *the establishment of authentic fraternity."*[48]

In order to properly understand the principle of gratuitousness, one needs first to understand the meaning of fraternity, and what distinguishes authentic from false or reductive notions of fraternity. *Caritas in Veritate* is directed at the same time to the Christian faithful as well as all people of good will; but it is unlikely that these groups would grasp fraternity in the same way, or should determine similar ways for reforming human relations.[49] Driven by the charity

---

[47] *Spe Salvi*, 21.
[48] *Caritas in Veritate*, 20. (My emphasis).
[49] Title of the encyclical: Encyclical letter *Caritas in Veritate* of the Supreme Pontiff Benedict XVI to the Bishops, Priests and Deacons, Men and Women Religious, the Lay Faithful, and all People of Good Will on Integral Human Development in Charity and Truth.

of Christ, the Christian community would have a Christological understanding of fraternity, whilst the non-Christian people are more likely to embrace a more humanistic or anthropological understanding.

The Christological understanding of fraternity is concretized in the *Corporal Works of Mercy* to which Christ invites each person to respond, because to serve the other is to serve Christ himself. The corporal works of mercy constitute what authentic fraternity means. Fraternity means accountability and giving without requiring recompense. It is to feed the hungry, give drink to the thirsty, clothe the naked, shelter the homeless, visit the sick, visit the imprisoned, and bury the dead.[50] This is what charity in truth demands from authentic fraternity – care and love for the other. This Christological understanding echoes the Christ event of being 'for' the other. Vicarious representation is to be 'for' the other because of love.[51]

Benedict in *Spe salvi* notes how even St. Augustine of Hippo understood the mission of a Christian to be 'for the other', indeed 'for all'.

> After his conversion to the Christian faith, he decided, together with some like-minded friends, to lead a life totally dedicated to the word of God and to things eternal. His intention was to practice a Christian version of the ideal of the contemplative life expressed in the great tradition of Greek philosophy, choosing in this way the "better part" (cf. *Lk* 10:42). Things turned out differently, however. While attending the Sunday liturgy at the port city of Hippo, he was called out from the assembly by the Bishop and constrained to receive ordination for the exercise of the priestly ministry in that city. Looking back on that moment, he writes in his *Confessions*: **"Terrified by my sins and the weight of my misery, I had resolved in**

---
[50] Mt 25:34.
[51] Cf. Isaiah 53:11.

> my heart, and meditated flight into the wilderness; but you forbade me and gave me strength, by saying: 'Christ died for all, that those who live might live no longer for themselves but for him who for their sake died' (cf. 2 Cor 5:15)". **Christ died for all.** To live for him means allowing oneself to be drawn into his *being for others*.[52]

The Development of Christian Brotherhood

One could pursue a definition of fraternity as it developed historically, starting from the understanding of brotherhood in ancient Greece, in the Old Testament, to its development in Hellenism to the Enlightenment and Marxism. Additionally, one could pursue its definition from the words of Christ, and in the New Testament especially in St. Paul, in Early Christianity and then in the Fathers of the Church, as Cardinal Ratzinger undertakes in *The meaning of Christian Brotherhood*.[53] Lastly, one might attempt a definition from contemporary realities such as the phenomenon of globalization, political relationships and even ecumenical theology.

While pursuing this venture in search of a definition, it serves us well to base our research on the notion of fraternity made evident in the encyclical, *Caritas in Veritate*. Pope Benedict's understanding of fraternity is strikingly Christological: Jesus the Father's Son; and hence all Christians are brothers of Christ and brothers to one another by grace and adopted children of God. The introduction to the encyclical states that: "In Christ, *charity in truth* becomes the Face of his Person, a vocation for us to love our brothers and sisters in the truth of his plan. Indeed, he himself is the Truth (cf. *Jn* 14:6)."[54]

---

[52] *Spe Salvi*, 28. (Bold in the original)
[53] Cf. Joseph Ratzinger, *The Meaning of Christian Brotherhood* (San Francisco: Ignatius Press, 1993).
[54] *Caritas in Veritate*, 1.

In *The Meaning of Christian Brotherhood,* Ratzinger demonstrates how "brotherhood" developed in the Patristic era, when the Church Fathers established that it was by baptism that one was constituted to be a brother. "The word "brother" occurs frequently and as a matter of course in the Fathers up to the third century. Thus, it is baptism which is now regarded as the precise moment at which one becomes a "brother". It represents, as rebirth, the acceptance into the Christian 'brotherhood' as the community calls itself. In this rebirth the Church is the Mother and God is the Father."[55]

This notion of fraternity is seen particularly in the celebration of the Eucharist (the Eucharistic meal of brotherhood) where communion is made visible, hence, to speak of 'separated brothers' causes a problem. The Eucharistic celebration as a source of brotherhood (*adelphotes*) in the Church (*ekklesia*) is the answer to the question of a Christian humanism that leads to an integral human development – unity with Christ demands unity with the Christian community. "Like the fatherhood of God, the brotherhood of Christians in the Lord is raised – through the Christ-event-above the realm of ideas to the dignity of true actuality."[56] At the same time the Eucharist makes visible the true fraternal bond between people, and this is externally manifested by the community that gathers together in the celebration of the Eucharist.

The Eucharist is therefore the sacrament of unity that also gives direction to the realization of fraternity; it is the source of love and development. The economical, sociological and political world cannot be fraternal if the source is not in God the Father who manifests his love over and over again by giving Himself to humanity in Jesus the bread of

---

[55] Joseph Ratzinger, *The Meaning of Christian Brotherhood* (San Francisco: Ignatius Press, 1993), 37.
[56] Joseph Ratzinger, *The Meaning of Christian Brotherhood* (San Francisco: Ignatius Press, 1993), 50.

life, so that all may eat and have life within them. By being fed with Jesus the bread of life and the author of life, we become Christ-like and, in turn, feed our brothers and sisters who hunger for food, for justice and for the basic necessities of life. The Eucharistic perspective for development makes real the aspect of receiving and giving gratuitously; it is grace at work in the world.

FRATERNITAS ET GRATIA

Philipp Renczes[57] notes that "'grace' appears three times in the encyclical's introduction, where it is closely tied to 'love'. However, in *Deus caritas est*, which focuses entirely on 'love', 'grace' is referenced only twice, towards the end[58], both in rather specific contexts: first to illustrate the right attitude of the faithful, namely, as God's servant; then to highlight the eminent role of the Mother of God." Renczes continues: "[w]hile Benedict prefers to appeal to the more accessible notion of 'gift' when referring to ideas essential to the concept of grace, in fact his focus on 'grace' at the beginning (nos. 1-9), middle (no. 34), and end (no. 78) positions 'grace' as the encyclical's very framework."[59]

It is interesting how Renczes sees grace as the encyclical's very framework; however, it seems incomplete to single out grace without the notions of fraternity, subsidiarity, solidarity, and communion – notions which hold the encyclical together under the umbrella of 'integral human development.' It should be noted that no. 34 of the encyclical, as Renczes also alludes, states that "*Charity in truth* places man before the astonishing experience of gift…Gift by its nature goes beyond merit, its rule is that of superabundance."[60] It

---

[57] Professor of the Theology of Grace at the Pontifical Gregorian University, Rome.
[58] Cf. *Deus caritas est*, 35, 42.
[59] Philipp Renczes, *Grace Reloaded: Caritas in Veritate's Theological Anthropology* (Theological Studies 71, June 2010), 280. (footnotes 22 and 23).
[60] *Caritas in Veritate*, 34.

is only in this particular thought that grace might be taken to be the underlying key to the understanding of fraternity in its dimension of demanding gratuity in relationships.

Benedict XVI does not elaborate the definition of fraternity from the ecclesiological or the '*de gratia*' perspective but solely through the anthropological dimension in search of a true humanism, which, of course, if it is to be a true humanism has to be a Christian humanism. Nevertheless, the anthropological dimension finds its true identity in Christ, the perfect man, who reveals man's perfect state and endows him with grace.

The notion of fraternity in *Caritas in Veritate* does not, as well, delve into the Eucharistic mystery (as our incorporation in the one Body of Christ), but explores other notions that are imperative for development. *Caritas in Veritate* seeks a fraternity between all peoples of different race, culture, religion while having the Gospel as the great teacher of truth and love. Thus, fraternity cannot be analyzed apart from notions such as *communio, subsidiaritas, societas,* and *solidaritas* which are prevalent in the whole encyclical, particularly in Chapter Three: "Fraternity, economic development and civil society."

The notion of fraternity as Benedict understands it, cannot be understood apart from the notions of truth and love. "The human community that we build by ourselves can never, purely by its own strength, be a fully fraternal community, nor can it overcome every division and become a truly universal community. The unity of the human race, a fraternal communion transcending every barrier, is called into being by the word of God-who-is-Love."[61] *Veritas* and *caritas* are characteristic of God's being and therefore important for an understanding of fraternal incorporation into the Trinitarian communion.

---

[61] *Caritas in Veritate*, 34.

THE LOGOS OF GOD

The 'Word of God-who-is-Love' is Christ the Logos of God. Benedict does not speak here of particular truths (*logoi*) that are necessary for development, but rather of the foundation that constitutes a true communion of love. The encyclical, in fact, begins by laying out the theology of "Logos-creation" and "Logos-Redemption" that is superior to rational truths (*logoi*) that have often been elevated to subdue the supernatural. "Charity in truth, to which Jesus Christ bore witness by his earthly life and especially by his death and resurrection, is the principal driving force behind the authentic development of every person and of all humanity" (1).

Fraternity and grace are inseparable, because they are based on 'relationship', 'gratuity', and 'reciprocity'; "...men and women become subjects of charity, they are called to make themselves instruments of grace, so as to pour forth God's charity and to weave networks of charity" (5). By this reciprocity then, development (*gratia elevans*) becomes a mutual process of growth (*gratia co-operans*), that considers both the spiritual life and the human condition of man. "Development requires attention to the spiritual life, a serious consideration of the experiences of trust in God, spiritual fellowship in Christ, reliance upon God's providence and mercy, love and forgiveness, self-denial, acceptance of others, justice and peace" (79).

To open oneself to another means that one views the other as a brother, it is giving a gift gratuitously and receiving gratuitously the other's fraternal love – it is realizing what *gratia praeveniens* means, God interacting with man and man interacting with other people. John Paul II in *Centesimus annus* stated that, "[M]an cannot give himself to a purely human plan for reality, to an abstract ideal or to a false utopia. As a person, he can give himself to another person or to other persons, and ultimately to God, who is the author of his being and who alone can fully accept his gift."[62] Christ, the logos of God offers himself (also known as vicarious representation), so that man may be redeemed and in turn give himself selflessly to others as a kind of oblation.

In his introduction to *The Church and development in Africa*, Stan Chu Ilo indicates how opening oneself to others is crucial for development.

> The challenge of the modern world is the imprisonment to one narrative: seeing myself as the beginning and end of all things makes me a slave to myself and robs me of the thrill and expansive grace of stepping into the stories and worlds of others. If a nation closes itself to other nations, it becomes a slave to its own ideologies, its own limitations, and the pretensions of self-sufficiency, thereby losing the measuring rod and corrective and creative expansion that it could have gained from other nations.[63]

Closing oneself in deprives grace a place in one's life. This is a result of original sin, as Benedict observes, and it affects human relations if not recognized and healed. "Ignorance of the fact that man has a wounded nature inclined to evil gives rise to serious errors in the areas of education, politics, social action and morals."[64] Therefore, the notion of fraternity paves the way to understanding anthropology, introducing the notion of grace to heal human nature, and leads to a more sociological understanding of how people ought to interact in the world for an integral human development. The model of a total and gratuitous self-giving (oblation) is Christ the logos of God.

---

[62] *Centesimus Annus*, 41.
[63] Stan Chu Ilo, *The Church and development in Africa* (Oregon: Pickwick Publications, 2011), xxix.
[64] *Caritas in Veritate*, 34.

FRATERNITAS ET COMMUNIO

Fraternity and communion, founded on truth, pave the way to the dialogue that Benedict initiates between faith and reason. "*Truth*, in fact, is *logos* which creates *dialogos*, and hence communication and communion" (4). Reason by itself is not able to create fraternal community and is unable to lead to integral human development. Reason needs the fundamental values of truth and love in order to aid man in the pursuit of happiness and fraternity. On the other hand, reason also needs faith because both *fides et ratio* can be analogically seen as two lungs of humanity[65] seeking true fraternity and authentic development. Fraternity apart from communion cannot be authentic, for brotherhood is a communion of people gathered together by the values of love, truth and transparency.

Veritas, complementary to *Caritas*, is the light that will enlighten reason, and give meaning and value to charity. "[T]ruth is the light that gives meaning and value to charity. That light is both the light of reason and the light of faith, through which the intellect attains to the natural and supernatural truth of charity: it grasps its meaning as gift, acceptance, and communion" (3). Benedict here makes a distinction between the Truth as Logos/the Son of God, and particular truths which cannot exist apart from their source who is the *Logos par excellence*.

The Truth is a person, and truths are particular to a person who embraces them. Once a person embraces the Truth, who is Christ, therefore cannot refuse the particular truth of justice, peace, accountability, integrity, and what constitutes authentic Christian living such as putting into practice the corporal works of mercy.

---

[65] *Africae Munus*, 13. Cf. Benedict XVI, Homily at the Opening Mass of the Second Special Assembly for Africa of the Synod of Bishops (Vatican City: St. Peter's Basilica, 4 October 2009).

The ultimate goal in creating a fraternal community is to live together as caring brothers and sisters to one another," being my brother's keeper," that is, being accountable for others. Accountability goes hand-in-hand with fraternity, because fraternity demands accountability in human relations, economics and all that involves the human person. St. John Chrysostom eloquently stated what accountability is in regard to the needy:

> You eat to excess; Christ eats not what he needs. You eat a variety of cakes; he eats not even a piece of dried bread. You drink fine Thracian wine; but on him you have bestowed so much as a cup of cold water. You lie on a soft and embroidered bed; but he is perishing in the cold…You live in luxury on things that properly belong to him. Why, were you the guardian of a child and, having taken control of his estate, you neglected him in his extreme need, you would have ten thousand accusers and you would suffer the punishment set by law. At the moment, you have taken possession of the resources that belong to Christ and you consume them aimlessly. Don't you realize that you are going to be held accountable?[66]

This exhortation from John Chrysostom can be likened to the story told by Jesus about the rich man who had all the material needs in this world while Lazarus was poor but inherited eternal life.[67] Lazarus is depicted, in Luke's Gospel, as Christ in the poor; where the words "whatsoever you do to the least of my brothers, you do it to me", become a reality.

Nonetheless, what Luke communicates here is that the unjust will not only be held accountable before the world and punished only by human law, but will also be held

---

[66] John Chrysostom. Cf. Stan Chu Ilo, *The Church and Development in Africa* (Oregon: Pickwick Publications, 2011), xxiii.
[67] Lk 16:19-31.

accountable before God the Supreme Judge. Therefore, accountability should not only be seen as a necessity in this world having to observe human laws, but has to also be viewed in the eschatological sense where Divine justice has to be implemented correctly in the world because "it is right and just."

All authority comes from God; therefore, to fear judgment in this world and not have a focus on divine judgment is to have a narrow and incomplete focus to life. Life can be seen in two spheres, and these are in Augustinian terms: the *Civitas Dei* and the *Civitas terrena*. Life on earth can also be seen as a pilgrimage (*civitas Dei peregrina*) where the journey is towards eternal life in heaven.[68]

In the Gospel of Luke 16, the rich man neglects the poor man and does not pay any heed to the needy. However, at the end of the earthly pilgrimage the poor attain the Kingdom of God while the rich, who fail to see Christ in the poor, suffer torment in hell fire. Joseph Ratzinger reminds us in *Eschatology* to imitate the piety of the saints who labored not only for the salvation of their own souls but for the salvation of the souls of the whole world.

> For the saints, 'Hell' is not so much a threat to be hurled at other people but a challenge to oneself. It is a challenge to suffer in the dark night of faith, to experience communion with Christ in solidarity with his descent into the Night. One draws near to the Lord's radiance by sharing his darkness. One serves the salvation of the world by leaving one's own salvation behind for the sake of others.[69]

Although aid to the needy is a temporal affair of the earthly realm, it nevertheless has an eschatological dimension. It is

---

[68] Cf. Augustine, (R.W. Dyson ed.) *The City of God against the Pagans* (Cambridge: Cambridge University Press, 2002).

[69] Joseph Ratzinger, *Eschatology* (Washington, D.C.: CUA PRESS: 1988), 217-218.

not, however, out of fear of hell fire that justice has to be practiced in the world, but because of the love and need to be in communion with God and with our brothers and sisters when the earthly pilgrimage has come to an end.

THE PHENOMENON OF GLOBALIZATION

Trinitarian Communion is the communion within which our fraternal communion should find a place, because as Benedict states, "God desires to incorporate us into this reality of communion as well: 'that they may be one even as we are one' (*Jn* 17:22)."[70] However openness to inter into the Trinitarian communion is required, so that one may participate fully in the life of the other, eradicating superficiality, the selfish exchange of gifts, and ultimately eradicating underdevelopment (39).

Although in order for fraternal communion to materialize, the phenomenon of globalization has to be considered. This phenomenon "*a priori*, is neither good nor bad. It will be what people make of it" (42).[71] Therefore, fraternity and communion need not only be understood theologically but sociologically as well, considering the changes in society especially as society faces the multifaceted and complex phenomenon of globalization (42).

When globalization is viewed positively, not just as an unexpected phenomenon, then it is able to create true communion of brethren, rather than of neighbors who live next to each other. "*The development of peoples depends, above all, on a recognition that the human race is a single family* working together in true communion, not simply a group of subjects who happen to live side by side" (53). The Father, the Son, and the Holy Spirit are always united and are not persons living side by side.

---

[70] *Caritas in Veritate*, 54.
[71] Cf. John Paul II, *Address to the Pontifical Academy of Social Sciences*, 27 April 2001.

Humanity, therefore, ought to imitate the Trinitarian communion of love that exists in the Trinity.

The negative side of globalization is to take this phenomenon as plainly sociological and not regard it as a phenomenon that affects all aspects of life: culture, religion, economics and politics. To live together in communion means that I enter into the life of the other, and my views are shaped by the interaction I have with the other. It is a creation of the 'I-Thou' relationship rather than an unrelated 'I-Thou' relationship. On a vertical level, it is my relationship with God that shapes the horizontal level, which is my relationship with others, to be authentic and life-giving.

Certain cultures have developed the notion of fraternity within communion and express this notion as *Ubuntu*[72] which properly understood means humanism. Therefore, communion is not void of fraternity and not void of a true humanism. However, there are ethnic cultures that refuse to enter into communion with others from different ethnic groups, as described in the next section. At the same time, as Benedict notes, there are even "religious cultures in the world today that do not oblige men and women to live in communion but rather cut them off from one other (*sic*) in a search for individual well-being, limited to the gratification of psychological desires."[73]

GLOBALIZATION AND CULTURE

The Nigerian writer Chinua Achebe, in his *Things fall Apart* tells the story of the arrival of missionaries in Africa, and also tells the story of how local Christian ministers have sought to transform the traditions in Nigeria. For example,

---

[72] *Ubuntu* – a Nguni word meaning humanism/'personhood'.
[73] *Caritas in Veritate*, 55.

in Okwonkwo's tribe, twins were banished and any handicapped child was thrown into the evil forest to die. One Christian minister (Mr. Kiaga) had his church built on the edge of the evil forest and the village. This is like creating a point of convergence between good and evil. It is a replica of Golgotha, where Christ is crucified outside the city walls but where he can be seen by those coming into the city as a man crucified amongst criminals. However, the cross becomes the means to salvation, of reconciliation for the crucified and the perpetrators.

> There is also Mr. Kiaga's church in Mbata that welcomes slaves and other social outcasts in their midst and rescues twins from the Evil Forest. All in all, Mr. Kiaga's church lives by and encourages gentleness, hospitality, affection, service, and even humility – the very same qualities Umuofia dismisses as women's characteristics or signs of weakness…Here in the outskirts of the fierce competition for domination and invincibility, Mr. Kiaga's church is able to nurture and sustain those values and qualities that Mr. Smith's church could not. In the end, the virtues of hospitality, care, and gentleness reflect a different form of politics, and thus offer an alternative to the competition for domination at the center of Umuofia's village life.[74]

St. Augustine in his 'City of God' makes a distinction between the elect who are members of the *civitas Dei*; those who are not chosen by God are members of the *civitas terrena* and are destined to eternal damnation. To live in the *civitas Dei* means that God has favored the members and given his graces to them, and their end is eternal life not damnation.[75]

---

[74] Emmanuel, Katongole, *The Sacrifice of Africa – A Political Theology for Africa* (Cambridge, Wm. B. Eerdmans Publishing Co.: 2011), 130.
[75] Cf. Augustine, (R.W. Dyson ed.) *The City of God against the Pagans* (Cambridge: Cambridge University Press, 2002), Book XIV, 13.

It is love that unites the two cities according to Augustine – love of God or love of self. With Okwonkwo's tribe, it is either love of humanity that promotes life or love of one's culture that promotes death. The love of humanity seen in the reconciliation of good and evil can properly be called love of God. However, the love of one's culture that promotes the killing of the innocent is not based on authentic love but on a false premise of what love ought to be.[76]

FRATERNITAS ET SUBSIDIARITAS

Fraternity and subsidiarity have a huge place in the whole encyclical, and are always connected, not just as notions but as fundamental principles like those of charity and truth. However, *subsidiaritas* is also closely linked to *solidarietas* throughout the encyclical.

Although Benedict underlines the centrality of the human person, he also emphasizes the centrality of Christ within the human person. "In *development programmes,* the principle of the *centrality of the human person,* as the subject primarily responsible for development, must be preserved."[77] It is interesting to note here that Benedict seems to be moving in the direction of an anthropological humanism, rather than a Christological humanism; whether the dependency for human development should be placed in the human person or in God or simultaneously in both is not clear in this regard. However, anthropology properly understood, linked to fraternity, is the key to embracing the principles of solidarity and subsidiarity.

On the issue of bioethics, for example, Benedict is clear that it "is no coincidence that closing the door to transcendence brings one up short against a difficulty: how could being emerge from nothing, or how could intelligence be born

---

[76] Cf. Augustine, (R.W. Dyson ed.) *The City of God against the Pagans* (Cambridge: Cambridge University Press, 2002), Book XIV, 13.
[77] *Caritas in Veritate,* 47.

from chance?" (74). Therefore, even in this regard there is need for dialogue between faith and reason not a separation.

> Subsidiary respects personal dignity by recognizing in the person a subject who is always capable of giving something to others. By considering reciprocity as the heart of what it is to be a human being, subsidiarity is the most effective antidote against any form of all-encompassing welfare state. It is able to take account both of the manifold articulations of plans – and therefore of the plurality of subjects – as well as the coordination of those plans. Hence the principle of subsidiarity is particularly well-suited to managing globalization and directing it towards authentic human development. (57)

Benedict defines subsidiarity as "first and foremost a form of assistance to the human person via the autonomy of intermediate bodies" (57). Subsidiarity is from the Latin word *subsidium* meaning to help or support. Nevertheless, *"[t]he principle of subsidiarity must remain closely linked to the principle of solidarity and vice versa,* (sic) since the former without the latter gives way to social privatism, while the latter without the former gives way to paternalist social assistance that is demeaning to those in need" (58).

Stefano Zamagni has stated that while a fraternal society is also a society of solidarity, it is not necessarily true that a society of solidarity is a fraternal society: *"Il fatto è che mentre la società fraterna è anche una società solidale, il viceversa non è necessariamente vero."*[78]

Just as globalization is an issue between fraternity and communion, so is it for fraternity and subsidiarity. It is true that globalization has to be properly managed, not only because it proves to be either good or bad but because it is a

---

[78] Stefano Zamagni, *Fraternità, Dono, Reciprocità nella 'Caritas in Veritate'* (Università di Bologna: Ottobre 2009).

growing phenomenon of the current century. "The integral development of people and international cooperation require the establishment of a greater degree of international ordering, marked by subsidiarity, for the management of globalization."[79] An authority that would monitor the progress of the phenomenon of globalization is needed, so that human freedom is not infringed upon and that the common good is sought.

> In order not to produce a dangerous universal power of a tyrannical nature, *the governance of globalization must be marked by subsidiarity* (sic), articulated into several layers and involving different levels that can work together. Globalization certainly requires authority, insofar as it poses the problem of a global common good that needs to be pursued. This authority, however, must be organized in a subsidiary and stratified way, if it is not to infringe upon freedom and if it is to yield effective results in practice. (57)

One of the principles that Benedict offers as an option for economic distribution is the use of fiscal subsidiarity. "One possible approach to development aid would be to apply effectively what is known as fiscal subsidiarity, allowing citizens to decide how to allocate a portion of the taxes they pay to the State. Provided it does not degenerate into the promotion of special interests, this can help to stimulate forms of welfare solidarity from below, with obvious benefits in the area of solidarity for development as well" (60). The principles offered by Benedict, such as subsidiarity, aim at the development of the human person and at the positive wellbeing of a globalized society.

---

[79] *Caritas in Veritate*, 67.

Fraternitas in Societas

The notion of fraternity or of reciprocity within society demands justice, charity and truth for the creation of a just society. As Benedict has noted: "*Ubi societas, ibi ius:* every society draws up its own system of justice. *Charity goes beyond justice,* because to love is to give, to offer what is 'mine' to the other; but it never lacks justice, which prompts us to give the other what is 'his', what is due to him by reason of his being or his acting" (6).

The human person through birth enters into a humanity marked by original sin. The fall of Adam and Eve is not an event to be solely regarded as historical but as characteristic of humanity; man is born just and at the same time sinful. Society cannot deny original sin. To deny that humankind is marked by sinful nature and is forever inclined to sin, even though grace is given, would be incorrect.

The consequences of original sin are evident even today because man is still inclined to search for selfish means of satisfying himself in a consumerist society. It is therefore necessary for man to discover the gifts of truth and charity which impose themselves on all. The theological virtues of faith, hope and charity are gifts that drive us to seek to do the good and avoid the wrong (34).

The global market, for example, is an encounter in society in which people come together; it is a place of reciprocity – fraternity. However, it could also be a platform of manipulation and a way of promoting the consumerist culture of seeking one's own good while others suffer the lack of freedom and the opportunity to progress.

The best form of justice that could be practiced in society is therefore distributive justice, where relations on a larger scale, help to create equality and will eradicate the inequality that exists between the rich and the poor. When the market is understood as a mechanical platform in which the priority is not 'people in relation' but objects (such as money), then each person will seek his own good and the virtues of truth and justice will cease to be maintained. "In and of itself, the market is not, and must not become, the place where the strong subdue the weak. Society does not have to protect itself from the market, as if the development of the latter were *ipso facto* to entail the death of authentic human relations" (36).

Fraternity in society reminds us of the need to work for the common good, and this is the duty of all people and not just of economics; politics have a role to play too as Benedict reminds us. "Economic activity cannot solve all social problems through the simple application of *commercial logic*. This needs to be *directed towards the pursuit of the common good,* for which the political community in particular must also take responsibility" (36).

The famous saying "money makes the world goes round", cannot be condoned because it is human relations in all its many dimensions that make life beautiful and fraternal. Fraternity is a good for human relations, without which human persons will only be interacting as objects void of the natural gifts of liberty and human dignity (36). Therefore, fraternity in society is imperative for the development of the human person. Society cannot avoid the role played by economics, politics, religion, and just systems that seek to elevate man from the status of being a victim of greed and injustice.

Fraternitas et Solidarietas

Responsibility is a virtue and cannot be lacking in the principle of solidarity, because solidarity seems to transform the 'unequal' to be 'equal' in society. "Solidarity is first and foremost a sense of responsibility on the part of everyone with regard to everyone…" (38). Stefano Zamagni in his article *Fraternità, Dono, Reciprocità nella 'Caritas in Veritate'*, underlined how the notion of fraternity once present in the flag of the French Revolution, and that found its true meaning in Franciscan thought, is properly to constitute the completion and elevation of the principle of solidarity.[80]

It is Christianity that has changed the whole notion of fraternity from being a mere notion of blood relations or a brotherhood of compatriots, to being a fraternity of all. Fraternity as it is in Christianity is a brotherhood of all peoples, made in the image and likeness of God the Father, and this gift finds its realization in Jesus Christ – the perfect revelation of God. It is therefore the paternity of God that characterizes the fraternity that exists among his children, made brothers because they are one with Christ the Son of God. In Jesus, all are made equal and 'all are responsible for all'.[81]

Solidarity is ontologically embedded in the nature of every human person. Man and woman, for example, complement one another ontologically and not only physically or psychologically. Together they form a community of love and solidarity.[82] It is self-centeredness that distances man from being in communion with the other – embracing an autonomous form of life. Solidarity is an authentic moral virtue; *The Compendium of the Social Doctrine of the Church* reminds us that this principle is "a *firm and persevering*

---

[80] Cf. Stefano Zamagni, *Fraternità, Dono, Reciprocità nella 'Caritas in Veritate'* (Università di Bologna: Ottobre 2009). *La parola chiave che oggi meglio di ogni altra esprime questa esigenza è quella di fraternità, parola già presente nella bandiera della Rivoluzione Francese, ma che l'ordine post-rivoluzionario ha abbandonato – per le note ragioni – fino alla sua cancellazione dal lessico politico-economico. È stata la scuola di pensiero francescana a dare a questo termine il significato che esso ha conservato nel corso del tempo. Che è quello di costituire, ad un tempo, il complemento l'esaltazione del principio di solidarità. Infatti mentre la solidarità è il principio di organizzazione sociale che consente ai diseguali di diventare eguali, il principio di fraternità è quell principio di organizzazione sociale che consente agli eguali di essere diversi. La fraternità consente a persone che sono eguali nella loro dignità e nei loro diritti fondamentali di esprimere diversamente il loro piano di vita, o il loro carisma.*

[81] Cf. Joseph Ratzinger, *The Meaning of Christian Brotherhood* (San Francisco: Ignatius Press, 1993).

[82] Cf. Pontifical Council for Justice and Peace, *Compendium of the Social Doctrine of the Church*, (Città del Vaticano, Libreria Editrice Vaticana: 2004).

determination to commit oneself to the *common good*. That is to say to the good of all and of each individual, because we are *all* really responsible *for all*" (193).

The Logic of Gift

The logic of gift can be summed up by the Gospel text, "Whatever you wish that men should do to you, do so to them."[83] This text incorporates the individual person with other people – it is a community of authentic relationships. Evidently, even though the relationship between persons does exist, there still exists unfair ways of giving and/or of receiving gifts.

The system of 'contract' has also created an unjust way of being in relation, where people make a contract with those who are unable to fulfill all that the contract demands. For example, to make a contract with one who is unable to respect it means that the contract is based on dishonesty and a lack of transparency. Therefore, the logic of gift calls persons to put into practice the values of transparency, honesty and above all charity in truth.

> The great challenge before us, accentuated by the problems of development in this global era and made even more urgent by the economic and financial crisis, is to demonstrate, in thinking and behavior, not only that traditional principles of social ethics like transparency, honesty and responsibility cannot be ignored or attenuated, but also that in *commercial relationships* the *principle of gratuitousness* and the logic of gift as an expression of fraternity can and must *find their place within normal economic activity*. This is a human demand at the present time, but it is also demanded by economic logic. It is a demand both of charity and of truth.[84]

---

[83] Mt 7:12.
[84] *Caritas in Veritate*, 36.

Benedict speaks of the logic of gift as an expression of fraternity that needs to find its place within normal economic activity (36). Linked to the logic of gift is the notion of justice or righteousness. This logic of gift is not only found in economic activity, but is firstly found in families, where parents and children have a familial relationship, brothers and sisters, and also between associations and countries. The collaboration between all these people is already putting into practice the logic of gift as an expression of fraternity – giving of myself to the other freely and the other giving himself freely to me creating the 'We' community founded on the Trinitarian communion love.

Benedict challenges us not only to remain a fraternal community in families or small entities, but in the public sphere as well. In a family, when a brother is dying of hunger, the brother who has enough is obliged by charity to share with the needy. However, in society today, the existence of hunger in the world is a failure on the part of all institutions. It is within family life that people come to learn what fraternity means, what giving selflessly means and what it means to co-exist happily knowing that the joy of another is my joy and the pain of the other is mine too. This is co-responsibility. However, if family life is not a starting point of teaching such values, it seems rather improbable to teach this on a larger platform such as in economic life.

Stefano Zamagni has rightly pointed out that the proper function of 'gift' is to understand that together with the gifts of justice there are also gratuitous gifts; therefore, no society is authentically human when it is satisfied by just the gifts of justice. However, it is necessary to ask what the difference is between the gifts of justice, and gratuitous gifts. He states that the gifts of justice find their source from a 'must', whereas the gifts of gratuity find their source from an 'obligation.'[85]

The revelation of God as love (1Jn 4:8) is the foundation of fraternity and is therefore the answer to the transformation of the world to be a brotherhood of love. The 'reform', sought by *Populorum Progressio,* is that of reforming all that is not love to authentic charity in authentic brotherhood. The gifts of justice and gratuity can only be realized when people grasp that they are interconnected in a fraternal way.

The authentic fraternal community that we seek is that spoken of by St. Paul, "There is neither Jew nor Greek, there is neither slave nor free, there is neither male nor female; for you are all one in Christ Jesus."[86] This exhortation to the Galatians, although directed to the Gentiles accepting Christianity, can be proclaimed to the whole world marked by inequalities and cultural, social, economic and religious divisions.

Fraternity is therefore communion, solidarity, unity – the realization of the relationship between all people who by grace are adopted sons and daughters of God. God in his love gives the gifts of truth and love to all so that all people may be agents of development. However, this development cannot take place apart from the gifts of charity and truth embedded in the heart of every person.

---

[85] Stefano Zamagni, *Fraternità, Dono, Reciprocità nella 'Caritas in Veritate'* (Università di Bologna: Ottobre 2009). *I beni di giustizia sono quelli che nascono da un dovere; i beni di gratuità sono quelli che nascono da una obbligatio. Sono beni cioè che nascono dal riconoscimento che io sono legato ad un altro, che, in un certo senso, è parte costitutiva di me...Ebbene, la CV ci sice che una società per ben funzionare e per progredire ha bisogno che all'interno della prassi economica ci siano soggetti, che capiscano cosa sono i beni di gratuità, che si capisca, in altre parole, che abbiamo bisogno di far rifluire nei circuiti della nostra società il principio di gratuità.*
[86] Gal 3:28.

Chapter Three

Fraternitas in Relation to Human Development

Development as Vocation

An anthropological understanding of the human person is vital in order to work at achieving human development. Human development without being centered on the human person is useless, and lacks focus. On the other hand, the human person cannot seek development solely by his own powers.[87] It is clear that Benedict by calling development a 'vocation' asserts that God cannot be disregarded, and the human communion based on solidarity cannot be disregarded as well (16-19).

> In reality, institutions by themselves are not enough, because integral human development is primarily a vocation, and therefore it involves a free assumption of responsibility in solidarity on the part of everyone. Moreover, such development requires a transcendent vision of the person, it needs God: without him, development is either denied, or entrusted exclusively to man, who falls into the trap of thinking he can bring about his own salvation, and ends up promoting a dehumanized form of development. (11)

When the person is viewed as solely the means and end of human development, capable of bringing about his own salvation, then man is trapped in a 'dehumanized form of development,' as Benedict affirms.

Benedict is not, however, the only one to call development a vocation. Paul VI also taught that progress is a vocation. In fact, Benedict connects *Caritas in Veritate* with *Populorum Progressio* and teaches that "Paul VI taught that

---

[87] CF. *Caritas in Veritate*, 11.

progress, in its origin and essence, is first and foremost a *vocation*: 'in the design of God, every man is called upon to develop and fulfill himself, for every life is a vocation'" (16).[88] Vocation in essence involves two subjects: God and man.

The Church as a community of believers puts the person at the center of development because man is made in the image and likeness of God; he carries within himself the true image of God, and is able to act in the likeness of God by love, hope, freedom, and virtues that promote the dignity of all human persons. By responding to God's call of development, man likewise discovers his true identity as a person living in solidarity with others.

The relationship between God and man cannot be broken by any institution let alone in the name of pursuing development. It is important to remember that Joseph Ratzinger in his *The Spirit of the Liturgy* reminded society of the importance of the recognition of God which in turn means the recognition of man.

> When human affairs are so ordered that there is no recognition of God, there is a belittling of man...God has a right to a response from man to man himself, and where that right of God totally disappears, the order of law among men is dissolved, because there is no cornerstone to keep the whole structure together.[89]

Vocation derives from God and therefore man has to consider the Divine in the pursuit of development in order to keep the structure of society intact - strengthened by fraternity and solidarity. Just as Christ offers an authentic humanism, in the same way there can never be an authentic

---

[88] Cf. *Populorum Progressio*, 15.
[89] Joseph Ratzinger, *The Spirit of the Liturgy* (San Francisco: Ignatius Press, 2000), 19.

humanism "but that which is open to the Absolute, and is conscious of a vocation which gives human life its true meaning."[90]

Fraternitas as Charity and Solidarity

Development, understood as a vocation, creates brotherhood between people and underdevelopment does not create brotherhood. Therefore, fraternity is the goal that should be sought by all people who respond to the vocation of development in a globalized world. Both charity and solidarity work at building a truly fraternal community that aims at the integral development of all peoples.

The understanding of fraternity as charity and as solidarity is an outstanding contribution to social thinking. For example, Benedict states that "the vision of development as a vocation brings with it the *central place of charity within that development*" (19). Here therefore, we see the need to connect fraternity and charity.

There is also the need to link fraternity to solidarity, especially in a globalized society. "Underdevelopment has an even more important cause than lack of deep thought: it is 'the lack of brotherhood among individuals and peoples'" (19). Of course, Paul VI was the first to point out the causes of underdevelopment. These causes, as he pointed out, are not primarily of the material order, but they include a lack of fraternity, a lack of charity and a lack of solidarity. Paul VI invited society to search for the causes of underdevelopment in various dimensions of the human person: "first of all, in the will, which often neglects the duties of solidarity; secondly in thinking, which does not always give proper direction to the will" (19).

In addition to Paul VI's observations, Benedict offers another dimension of the human person which has often been

---

[90] *Caritas in Veritate*, 16.

neglected – the human soul. Benedict is clear in his teaching that as much as development is not only based on the material order, it is also closely bound to the spiritual order. *"The question of development is closely bound up with our understanding of the human soul, insofar as we often reduce the self to the psyche and confuse the soul's health with emotional well-being"* (76).

Although the encyclical is directed to all people, Benedict does not shy from speaking of the human person as composed of body and soul. In a globalized society where spirituality has often been degraded and the soul disregarded, Benedict returns to teach about the place of the soul in human life. This emphasis on the soul is also found in *Eschatology*, where Joseph Ratzinger refutes the claim of the nonexistence of the soul and the fear of facing death.[91]

The 'theology of the soul' is not solely a doctrine of Christianity but is part of humanity, and therefore Benedict offers this teaching to all people who strive not only for development but for an authentic humanism as well.

> *Development must include not just material growth but also spiritual growth,* since the human person is a 'unity of body and soul', born of God's creative love and destined for eternal life. The human being develops when he grows in the spirit, when his soul comes to know itself and the truths that God has implanted deep within, when he enters into dialogue with himself and his Creator.[92]

The contribution that Benedict offers to social teaching, and to the observations made by Paul VI, is that development must include both material growth and spiritual growth, but never just material growth. We can therefore affirm that social teaching cannot disregard theology because if

---

[91] Cf. Joseph Ratzinger, *Eschatology* (Washington D.C.: CUA Press, 1988).
[92] *Caritas in Veritate*, 76.

doctrines such as the Trinity or even the theology of the soul are not inserted in social thought then social teaching risks existing in a vacuum.

PAUL VI AND *FRATERNITAS* AS CHARITY AND SOLIDARITY

Paul VI, like Benedict found charity and solidarity to be at the core of the pursuit for progress/development. Charity and solidarity are therefore necessary to building a truly fraternal community based on honesty, transparency and truth. The solutions that Paul VI offered in solving the problems of underdevelopment and the attacks of hunger, deprivation, endemic diseases and illiteracy were:

> From the economic point of view, this meant their active participation, on equal terms, in the international economic process; from the social point of view, it meant their evolution into educated societies marked by solidarity; from the political point of view, it meant the consolidation of democratic regimes capable of ensuring freedom and peace.[93]

In a world that faces the phenomenon of globalization, we might ask whether it is possible to obtain all these solutions and attain brotherhood by human effort alone. Can reason alone, without faith, guarantee the pursuit of such development from the economic point of view, the social point of view, and from the political point of view? We find the answer in the one who gives the vocation to man and leaves him the freedom to respond; it is God who calls and teaches us 'through the Son what fraternal charity is' (19). Only God can offer helpful solutions to the world's problems, and the solutions can be translated from Scripture, by man who lives a truly authentic Christian humanism.

---

[93] *Caritas in Veritate*, 21.

Paul VI laid the foundation to understanding development from both the material order and the spiritual order. His sense of the *cultus hominis* is what can be regarded as the gateway to viewing development anthropologically, taking man not solely as a 'body' that needs to progress for survival but as a 'composed being of body and soul. In this sense then, development as a vocation is clearly connected to its origin – God. By regarding the irreplaceable role that God plays in development, solutions for development will truly be the fruits of man's response to the vocation received from God.

CULTUS HOMINIS, ACCORDING TO REASON AND METAPHYSICS[94]

Benedict is influenced by St. Augustine's understanding of truth – the truth of ourselves as given to us. In like manner, just as development is a vocation, so is the gift of truth that God gives to man. "Truth – which is itself gift, in the same way as charity – is greater than we are, as Saint Augustine teaches" (34). Man made in the image and likeness of God responds to this vocation so that he may be a true image of God.

The mention of *imago Dei* appears only once in the encyclical (45); nonetheless, it does not mean that Benedict does not promote the importance of being made in the image of God, as attested in *Gen* 1:27. The human person, *imago Dei*, is the most important and chief protagonist of human development when he responds to the vocation of development. Responding in charity and truth, man discovers the greatness of the God who has freely bestowed these gifts onto him; "Truth, like love, 'is neither planned nor willed, but somehow imposes itself upon human beings'" (34).

---

[94] *Caritas in Veritate*, Chapter 3.

Benedict relates humans to God through *caritas* and then relates development to *caritas*. For example, the very first parts of the encyclical's introduction are centered on how humans are related to God through the gift of *caritas*.[95] Later on in the encyclical, the relation of development to *caritas* is made with reference to the message that Benedict himself gave at the World Day of Peace, in the year 2008: "... 'after pondering responsibly the road to be taken, decisions aimed at strengthening that *covenant between human beings and the environment,* which should mirror the creative love of God, from whom we come and towards whom we are journeying'" (50).[96]

Man is also an important subject in the creation of the communion of persons (*communio personarum*). The human person has been created in love by God who is love - *Deus caritas est*; it is because of this love that the human person has also been entrusted with the prerogative of caring for creation and therefore seeing to its development.

Nevertheless, the human person has to find ways of developing as well, not just to focus development outside of himself (*ad extra*). To speak of developing trust in God and man is essential; "The idea of a world without development indicates a lack of trust in man and in God."[97]

Benedict XVI responds to the attacks that face the human person today. These attacks take the form of greed, poverty, war, terrorism, negative globalization, and the manipulation of the environment. Paul VI responded to the same attacks in *Populorum Progressio,* and his understanding of development was "rescuing peoples, first and foremost, from hunger, deprivation, endemic diseases and illiteracy" (21).[98]

---

[95] Cf. Ibid., 1-5.
[96] Cf. Benedict XVI, *Message for the 2008 World Day of Peace*, 7: AAS 100 (2008), 41.
[97] *Caritas in Veritate*, 14.
[98] Cf. *Populorum Progressio*.

The relationship between the human person and creation is one that has its source in God-who-is-love. The same Divine love is the same that ought to penetrate the person in order to fully participate in God's act of creation. Man, as *imago Dei*, is therefore capable of transmitting the love of God to all of creation by not manipulating it, but by working to its authentic development.

The human person needs to be understood from the aspect of being relational. "[T]he Christian revelation of the unity of the human race presupposes a *metaphysical interpretation of the 'humanum' in which relationality is an essential element.*"[99] The communion of persons is vital just as the communion of persons with creation is vital for human sustenance. This human sustenance is not only about being webbed in the natural food chain, but overcoming the tendency to think of man as an abstract being who might be living in the 'world of forms', to use Plato's phrase. It is here therefore that we can talk of sustainable development bearing in mind the relational communion between persons in the world.

BENEDICT'S METAPHYSICAL READING OF *HUMANUM* IN RELATION TO CULTURE

The human person, more than being rational, relational and made in the image and likeness of God, is also a cultural being. The human person is conditioned by the culture in which he finds himself. Therefore, when one finds himself in a culture that promotes isolation rather than communion, then one needs to transcend culture and opt for the communion revealed by the Triune God.

> Being in the image of God the human individual possesses the dignity of a person, who is not just something,

---

[99] *Caritas in Veritate*, 55.

but someone. He is capable of self-knowledge, of self-possession and of freely giving himself and entering into communion with other persons. Further, he is called by grace to a covenant with his Creator, to offer him a response of faith and love that no other creature can give in his stead.[100]

There are other cultural and religious issues that are a threat to true communion and to the dignity of the human person. Benedict calls these problems forms of 'syncretism.' "One possible negative effect of the process of globalization is the tendency to favor this kind of syncretism by encouraging forms of 'religion' that, instead of bringing people together, alienate them from one another and distance them from reality."[101]

Benedict continues this line of thought stating that, "some religious and cultural traditions persist which ossify society in rigid social groupings, in magical beliefs that fail to respect the dignity of the person, and in attitudes of subjugation to occult powers. In these contexts, love and truth have difficulty asserting themselves, and authentic development is impeded" (55).

These cultural and religious realities cannot contribute to authentic development let alone to the freedom of the human person and a true humanism. Christ is the response to development because the message he offers is one of truth in charity the pillars of integral human development. Culture therefore has to be imbedded in the respect of the human person capable of responding to the vocation of development and the creation of a culture of love and truth.

Culture runs the risk of cultural relativism where cultures exist side by side with no true integration but each promoting its own way of life. The philosophy of relativism

---

[100] *Catechism of the Catholic Church*, 357.
[101] *Caritas in Veritate*, 55.

has today become a hindrance to the understanding and implication of developmental structures. Relativism has become a hindrance as it is based on a self-centered pursuit for development rather than development as a pursuit of each and every human person.

The notion of fraternity cannot therefore be aligned with relativism, because fraternity opens man to others (Deut. 15: 7-8; Lev 19:33-34), whereas relativism locks man within himself and his culture. Human development entails the growth and success of the individual, however, not at the expense of the underdevelopment of the others. Fraternity opens the way to a journey together, where a proper humanism strives at the development of all and not solely of one.[102]

Benedict XVI states how truth needs to take the 'upper hand' in all the spectrums of life and this truth needs to be placed in the 'economy' of charity. "This is a matter of no small account today, in a social and cultural context which relativizes truth, often paying little heed to it and showing increasing reluctance to acknowledge its existence." [103] Here, Benedict links truth to charity and never separates them. It is as if to say, where there is truth without charity that truth cannot be authentic, and where there is charity without truth then that charity cannot be authentic. The spiritual thoughts of Blessed Columba Marmion (1858-1923) can help us understand the reasons why Benedict links charity and truth as means to development – our vocation.

> Is it enough that our acts are 'true', that they are in conformity with our condition as reasonable created beings subject to God, that they are freely carried out and are in

---

[102] Cf. Pontifical Council for Justice and Peace, *Compendium of the Social Doctrine of the Church*, (Città del Vaticano, Libreria Editrice Vaticana: 2004), 16.
[103] *Caritas in Veritate*, 2.

conformity with our state of life – is all this enough for them to be acts of super-natural life? No, that is not enough; they must, as well (and this is the chief point) proceed from grace – be carried out by a soul adorned with sanctifying grace. That is what St Paul means by his phrase 'in charity'.[104]

Relativism has somehow dressed superficiality with values of truth or charity in a deceiving way. The person therefore has to seek, find and express the truth within the economy of charity; otherwise, this will lead to moral irresponsibility, and selfish ends.

Without truth, without trust and love for what is true, there is no social conscience and responsibility, and social action ends up serving private interests and the logic of power, resulting in social fragmentation, especially in a globalized society at difficult times like the present.[105]

Paul, in his letter to the Ephesians, links truth to charity, but Benedict notes that we need "to link charity with truth not only in the sequence, pointed out by Saint Paul, of *veritas in caritate* (*Eph* 4: 15), but also in the inverse and complementary sequence of *Caritas in Veritate*" (2).

THE ENLIGHTENMENT OF REASON THAT COMES FROM CHRISTIAN REVELATION

Fraternity and Cooperation demand the inclusion-in-relation of all peoples so that one may talk of one community made up of individuals who are not mere neighbors but brothers and sisters to one another. Benedict states this clearly saying that "[t]he theme of development can be identified with the inclusion-in-relation of all individuals and

---

[104] Blessed C. Marmion, (Alan Bancroft trans.) *Christ, The Life of the Soul* (Herefordshire: Gracewing Publishing, 2005), 283.
[105] *Caritas in Veritate*, 5.

people within the one community of the human family, built in solidarity on the basis of the fundamental values of justice and peace" (54).

By promoting the notion of communion and then stating how this can be perfected by the Trinitarian communion, Benedict appeals to metaphysics and reason. "This perspective is illuminated in a striking way by the relationship between the Persons of the Trinity within the one divine Substance" (54).

Benedict's appeal to metaphysics and reason is to state his underlying theme that reason may be enlightened by faith. "Relationship between human beings throughout history cannot but be enriched by reference to this divine model. In particular, *in the light of the revealed mystery of the Trinity*, we understand that true openness does not mean loss of individual identity but profound interpenetration" (54).

GOD AS LOVE

In his first encyclical, *Deus caritas est*, Benedict states how important it is to grasp the true meaning of love. "God's love for us is fundamental for our lives, and it raises important questions about who God is and who we are. In considering this, we immediately find ourselves hampered by a problem of language. Today, the term "love" has become one of the most frequently used and misused of words, a word to which we attach quite different meanings."[106]

Benedict links the love of God with love of neighbor in both encyclicals: *Deus caritas est* and *Caritas in Veritate*. We can also observe how *Caritas in Veritate* continues the meaning of love developed in *Deus caritas est*. For example, an encounter with God guides man to discover the image of

---
[106] *Deus Caritas est*, 2.

God in the other and therefore work at loving and caring for that person. At the same time, an encounter with the God who is love produces a charitable encounter with others.

"Only through an encounter with God are we able to see in the other something more than just another creature, to recognize the divine image in the other, thus truly coming to discover him or her and to mature in a love that 'becomes concern and care for the other'" (11).[107] The theme of *imago Dei* returns again here, as noted that it is found explicitly mentioned once, in Chapter four (45).

GOD AS TRIUNE

Benedict links the fraternal communion of all people to the Trinitarian communion of the Father, the Son, and the Holy Spirit. The Triune God is three Persons united in the communion of love. Benedict affirms that the fraternal communion of people is 'illuminated' by the relationship between the Persons of the Blessed Trinity. Therefore, Benedict here introduces Trinitarian theology within the theme of development. "The reciprocal transparency among the divine Persons is total and the bond between each of them complete, since they constitute a unique and absolute unity."[108]

Fraternal communion would mean fraternal cooperation in which no individual loses his individual identity but by being open allows others to enter into communion with him. This is seen among spouses who give of themselves to one another and become 'one body.' At the same time, this is evident in true relationships between parents and children; there is a self-donation that takes place, and this self-donation reciprocally also means reception. This relationship is made more manifest in the mystery of the Trinity, in

---

[107] Cf. *Deus Caritas est,* 18.
[108] *Caritas in Veritate,* 54.

which, as Benedict states, "we understand that true openness does not mean loss of individual identity but profound interpenetration" (54).

CHRIST AS RECAPITULATION

Although the encyclical is directed to all peoples, not just to the Christian community, Benedict's main intent on speaking about Christ is derived from the use of reason, guided by faith, following an understanding of natural law which could be accepted by all. When Benedict invokes doctrines such as the Trinity and the recapitulation of creation in Christ, it is to show how beyond reasoning Christian teaching can cast new light on what reason provides.

Nevertheless, Benedict does not dismiss asking Christians to pray to God from whom authentic development derives. At the same time Benedict points to the eschatology of humanity – that all may pray to the Father in the words of Jesus. "[C]hristians long for the entire human family to call upon God as 'Our Father!' In union with the only-begotten Son, may all people learn to pray to the Father and to ask him, in the words that Jesus himself taught us..."[109]

The understanding of the human person is derived from Christology. It is Christ who is the full revelation of God. Christ is the New Man, "the 'last Adam [who] became a life-giving spirit' (*1 Cor.* 15:45), the principle of the charity that 'never ends' (*1 Cor. 13:8*)" (12). Man therefore, by striving to be more like Christ, embraces virtue and a life of grace and shuns sin and all that may lead to impairing the image of God – "Development requires attentions to the spiritual life, a serious consideration of the experiences of trust in God, spiritual fellowship in Christ, reliance upon God's providence and mercy, love and forgiveness, self-denial, acceptance of others, justice and peace" (79).

---

[109] *Caritas in Veritate*, 79.

Just as Benedict outlined development as a vocation, he also speaks of the importance of nature being 'recapitulated' in Christ at the end of time. "Nature speaks to us of the Creator (cf. *Rom* 1:20) and his love for humanity. It is destined to be 'recapitulated' in Christ at the end of time (cf. *Eph* 1:9-10; *Col* 1:19-20). Thus, it too is a 'vocation'" (48).

FRATERNITAS AT THE CORE OF THE UNDERSTANDING OF DEVELOPMENT

Fraternity is at the core of development, for a fraternal community is one that responds to the vocation of love, of truth and of development. All people are called to respond to this vocation, because it pertains to the human person. The Church, however, through its teaching and identity, reminds humanity of the need to place fraternity at the core of human development.

The mission of the Church is centered on the prerogative to heed the cry of the poor. The Church feels the sufferings of her members and of the entire world and is therefore called to respond in charity. Benedict XVI is clear as to what is the mission of the Church in the pursuit for integral human development. He states, "The Church does not have technical solutions to offer and does not claim 'to interfere in any way in the politics of States.' She does, however, have a *mission of truth* to accomplish, in every time and circumstance, for a society that is attuned to man, to his dignity, to his vocation."[110]

The Church, for Benedict, takes the place of Christ who as love is also 'for' the other. This Christological self-giving is what the members of the Church take upon themselves in order to aid the ones who are suffering. The Christological thought of 'vicarious representation', has been fully expounded by Joseph Ratzinger in his *Eschatology*. Benedict

---

[110] *Caritas in Veritate*, 9 (My emphasis).

offers the ecclesiological strength of vicarious representation whereas Ratzinger offers the Christological strength of this notion to be 'for' the other. Christ is 'for' the other, in the same way as the Church is 'for' the other with the hope of authentic human development.

> The nature of love is always to be "for" someone. Love cannot, then, close itself against others or be without them so long as time, and with it suffering, is real. No one has formulated this insight more finely than Thérèse of Lisieux with her idea of heaven as the showering down of love towards all. But even in ordinary human terms we can say, how could a mother be completely and unreservedly happy so long as one of her children is suffering?[111]

This notion of 'vicarious representation' is clearly seen towards the end of *Caritas in Veritate* where Benedict states: "God gives us the strength to fight and to suffer *for* love of the common good, because he is our All, our greatest hope."[112]

EXISTUS-REDITUS IN THE UNDERSTANDING OF DEVELOPMENT

Although the notion of *'exitus-reditus'* does not feature in the encyclical it nonetheless contributes to the understanding of development especially because of how Benedict links development to the Triune God. At the same time, *exitus-reditus* contributes to the assertion made by both Paul VI and Benedict XVI that development is a vocation. Therefore, it is important to understand what it means to relate development to God and to all human dimensions of body, soul and spirit.

Communion between mother and child is a good example of the natural bonds of authentic communion, stemming

---

[111] Joseph Ratzinger, *Eschatology* (Washington, D.C.: CUA PRESS, 1988), 188.
[112] *Caritas in Veritate*, 78 (My emphasis).

obviously from the umbilical interconnectedness. However, this communion is also realized by husband and wife brought together by bonds of affection. At the same time, the communion of persons is realized by the people and 'for' the people. There is also the communion between man and the Triune God. In a sense we can view the communion of persons as coming from (*exitus*) the Trinitarian communion and returning to (*reditus*) the Trinitarian communion.

The notions of *exitus-reditus* are also linked to the notion of fraternity and above all that of gift. Communion presupposes fraternity and gratuitous gift; this too echoes the theology of vicarious representation where there is a relationship 'for' and 'to'.

Joseph Ratzinger in *The Spirit of the Liturgy*, alludes to this theme when talking about sacrifices offered during worship. For example, Abraham instead of offering Isaac his son, is given a lamb by God to offer. "God gives the lamb, which Abraham then offers back to him."[113] This representative sacrifice is the expectation of Jesus who as the true lamb offers himself 'for' the many. He is the *Agnus Dei* who comes from God and returns to God. This can be seen in the theology of *exitus-reditus* – coming from and returning to (29-34).

Even in worship it is the human person who is at the center because God has no need of animal sacrifices. God is in need of mercy, love, and a contrite heart. In short the conversion of the heart, which is an authentic return to the Divine.

It is through discovering this notion of what man can give to God in worship that we can also discover what man can give to the world for development; gifts of love, mercy, justice, and truth contribute to a truly fraternal human community. When 'offering', as is understood in worship is

---

[113] Joseph Ratzinger, *The Spirit of the Liturgy*, 38.

embraced, then the human person can embark on an authentic development of all.

CATHOLIC SOCIAL TEACHINGS THAT SUPPLEMENT *CARITAS IN VERITATE*

The Catholic Church has for many years been referred to as *'phuthadichaba'*[114] in many mission territories, and this word has characterized the Catholic Church in Southern Africa, for example. *Phuthadichaba* means to gather the nations together. When people were living in great poverty, it was the Catholic Church that gave out food-parcels, clothing and basic human necessities to everyone irrespective of creed, culture and political status. This was not however, to take over the task of the State, but to provide where the state did not provide.

Benedict XVI does not only offer the encyclical *Caritas in Veritate* as the only proposal offered by the Church but also emphasizes the importance of Pope Paul VI's encyclical *Humanae vitae* (25 July 1968) and his apostolic exhortation *Evangelii nuntiandi* (December 8, 1975). These two documents, although not directly linked to social doctrine, offer helpful aids to human development. *Humanae vitae*, Benedict states, "emphasizes both the unitive and the procreative meaning of sexuality, thereby locating at the foundation of society the married couple, man and woman, who accept one another mutually, in distinction and complementarity: a couple, therefore, that is open to life ... *Humanae Vitae* indicates the *strong links between life ethics and social ethics*..."[115]

Here Benedict emphasizes the need to see human development as linked to the whole of man – body, soul, and spirit. Life ethics cannot be removed from social ethics,

---

[114] Sesotho name literally meaning to gather the nations, in its usage it means to gather all people together.
[115] *Caritas in Veritate*, 15.

because these are issues that are related and can never be divorced, not even by the philosophy of relativism that will emphasize life ethics as a personal affair in which society should not interfere. For example, abortion is not just a life ethics issue, but also a social issue involving not only the pregnant woman, but the child to be born, the father of the child, the family, the community, indeed the whole human family.

Conversely, separating life ethics from social ethics leads the human community to relativize and justify wrongdoing, incoherently speaking of *genus* and *species* to downgrade life ethics. A society that does this cannot be a fraternal community on the way to development. It is through evangelization, that the Church offers coherent teachings on such issues, either through encyclicals, preaching, engaging in Marches for life, as happens for example in Washington DC every year, or by handing out food-parcels as done in Southern Africa. This is why *Evangelii nuntiandi* is part of the *corpus* that Benedict offers in the search for solutions to human development. Paul VI stated that "evangelization would not be complete if it did not take account of the unceasing interplay of the Gospel and of man's concrete life, both personal and social."[116]

PASTORAL PERSPECTIVES TO DEVELOPMENT

Cardinal Peter Turkson, in his article *Caritas in Veritate: Good news for society* spoke about how the encyclical is good news for all people – be they in the slums or in very wealthy neighborhoods. Cardinal Turkson outlines the fact that *Caritas in Veritate,* among other factors, tries to help the weak so that they may not be subdued by the strong. Nevertheless, the weak need to know the language of Benedict

---

[116] *Evangelli Nuntiandi,* 29. Cf. *Caritas in Veritate,* 15.

in order to evidence the injustices present in their communities.

Cardinal Turkson gives an example of a young lady by the name of Rosanna[117] who, after being asked by Fr. Michael Czerney S.J., to whom the encyclical was directed, responded: 'to the whole world'. Rossana then added:

> I know the encyclical is about the whole world, but when I read the Pope's words, he is talking exactly about Kenya, even my slum. He says that the market must not become 'the place where the strong subdue the weak,' but it is. Billions of us live as neighbors to one another in our global village – or is it a global slum? – yet with too little fraternal relationship.[118]

It is through proposing solutions such as solidarity, subsidiarity, and fraternity that Benedict responds not only to global problems, but global problems that stem from the poorest of the poor. In a way we can say Benedict responds to the problems faced by the 'global slum,' to use Rossana's term. The response to these problems is driven by the need to create a fraternal community that will be built in charity and truth and that will eradicate the injustices that many people face.

Benedict XVI analogically sees the world as a respiratory organ. For example, at the opening Mass of the Second Synod for Africa (October 2009), he stated that "Africa constitutes an immense spiritual 'lung' for a humanity that appears to be in crisis of faith and hope."[119] Therefore, local and global social problems are a concern for the whole

---

[117] Rosanna is in her late twenties, she is HIV-positive and has one son Jomo; they live in a Nairobi slum.
[118] Cardinal Peter K.A. Turkson, *Caritas in Veritate: Good News for Society* (Article from Logos: A Journal of Catholic Thought and Culture, Volume 15, Number 3, Summer 2012), 90-108.
[119] Benedict XVI, *Homily* (Opening Mass of the Second Special Assembly for Africa of the Synod of Bishops: October 4, 2009).

world. Africa, as a continent suffers more socially, however it is a continent of hope in regard to the reception of the faith.

All people, regardless of where they find themselves geographically, need to form bonds of true communion; "interaction among the peoples of the world calls us to embark upon this new trajectory, so that integration can signify solidarity rather than marginalization."[120]

---

[120] *Caritas in Veritate*, 53.

Chapter Four

The Notion of *Fraternitas* in *Africae Munus*

AN ANALYSIS OF AFRICA'S COMMITMENT (*AFRICAE MUNUS*)

Africae Munus (Africa's commitment) is the fruit of the Second Special Assembly for Africa of the Synod of Bishops.[121] Properly called, it is a Post-Synodal Apostolic Exhortation of Pope Benedict XVI, promulgated in Benin on the 19th November 2011. Unlike encyclicals, particularly as evidenced in the analysis of *Caritas in Veritate,* the Post-Synodal Apostolic Exhortation has a particular audience – the Catholic community – and comes after many discussions and evaluations around a central theme.

The *Lineamenta, Instrumentum Laboris,* Synodal *relationes,* discussions, propositions voted, and the drafting committee, are the sources that lead to the Apostolic Exhortation.[122] *Africae Munus* is directed to the bishops, clergy, consecrated persons, and the lay faithful centered on the theme of "[T]he Church in Africa, in service to reconciliation, justice and peace."[123]

Fraternitas is a recurrent theme prevalent in *Caritas in Veritate* as already evidenced; it is also a theme that is central to *Africae Munus* proposed in an ecclesiological framework. In *Africae Munus,* Benedict provides proposals for commitment on how to create a brotherhood of love, whereas in *Caritas in Veritate* offers proposals on how to respond to the vocation of development, but since the audience is vast, he offers proposals that all of society can adopt, not just the Catholic community.

---

[121] I was present at all the gatherings of this Second Special Assembly for Africa of the Synod of Bishops, as assistant to the General Secretariat. (Vatican City: 4th – 25th October 2009).
[122] Cf. *Africae Munus,* 10.
[123] Text used: Official Latin and English text.

Nevertheless, in all cases Benedict maintains the character of being a moral voice, not only in the Catholic Church, but in society as did his predecessors, most noteworthy, Paul VI and John Paul II. It is Benedict's hope that Africa will live authentic fraternity and as a result be an example to the whole world. "[A]frica needs to hear the voice of Christ who today proclaims love of neighbor, love even of one's enemies, to the point of laying down one's life: the voice of Christ who prays today for the unity and communion of all people in God (cf. *Jn* 17:20-21)."[124]

In fact, Benedict states how his Apostolic Exhortation to Africa is linked, in thought and commitment, to John Paul II's Apostolic Exhortation *Ecclesia in Africa*. Indeed, as Benedict notes, *Ecclesia in Africa* "brought together the pastoral insights and proposals of the Synod Fathers for a new evangelization of the African continent" (2), which in continuity with this is what Benedict does through *Africae Munus*. The commitment involves the new evangelization of the African continent.

Fraternity in Benedict's analysis is at the service of the human person, as noted in *Caritas in Veritate*.[125] Fraternity is not void of love and truth (two primary principles of the vocation of development); this is where one notices the relationship between *Caritas in Veritate* and *Africae Munus*. The commitment of all peoples in the area of development is the commitment of love and truth. Africa's commitment is toward the human person in service of reconciliation, justice and peace anchored on charity and truth. For example, Benedict states:

> No society, however developed it may be, can do without fraternal service inspired by love. "Whoever wants to eliminate love is preparing to eliminate man as such.

---

[124] *Africae Munus*, 13.
[125] Cf. *Caritas in Veritate*, Chapter 3.

There will always be suffering which cries out for consolation and help. There will always be loneliness. There will always be situations of material need where help in the form of concrete love of neighbor is indispensable." It is love which soothes hearts that are hurt, forlorn or abandoned. It is love which brings or restores peace to human hearts and establishes it in our midst.[126]

Africae Munus can be analyzed by referring to the key themes that Pope Benedict points out; these key themes are Christology, Ecclesiology, Sacramentology, Anthropology, Eschatology, Pastoral Theology, and Human Development. These themes are in themselves ecclesiological because the audience of the apostolic exhortation is the Catholic community. These themes do not however lack an outreach to those who are not members of the Catholic Church. Ecclesiology has a pastoral dimension, especially that of the development of the human person as a child of God who needs to be placed in the freedom of knowing Christ, while at the same time being free to find means of responding to the vocation of development. The vocation of development is related in *Africae Munus* to reconciliation, justice and peace.

Evangelization is at the heart of the Church's mission, as *Ecclesia in Africa* sought to emphasize. By exhorting Africa towards a Christian commitment, African sociological issues have to be evaluated based on the Gospel and the Christian teaching of how-to live-in justice and peace – in service to the human person who has a vocation to development.

Africa has a lot to offer to the rest of the world, however in the midst of a crisis of faith, particularly in the Western world, the greatest gift that Africa can give is faith. When Joseph Ratzinger gave a lecture in the convent of Saint Scholastica in Subiaco (1st April 2005), he remembered the

---

[126] *Africae Munus*, 29. Cf. *Deus Caritas est*, 8.

recommendations of St. Benedict to his monks in order to get beyond the crisis of culture and reach God on High. In the same way, Africa can give these recommendations to the rest of the world so that authentic development centered on God can take place.

> Just as there is a bitter zeal that removes one from God and leads to hell, so there is a good zeal that removes one from vices and leads to God and to eternal life. It is in this zeal that monks must exercise themselves with most ardent love: May they outdo one another in rendering each other honor, may they support, in turn, with utmost patience their physical and moral infirmities...may they love one another with fraternal affection...Fear God in love...Put absolutely nothing before Christ who will be able to lead all to eternal life.[127]

What characterizes Benedict's document to Africa is the fact that he regards Africa as a continent of hope; at the same time, Benedict is sensitive to the wounds of Africa. Regardless of the terrible past that Africa carries, hope is what carries the continent forward. Benedict differs from many social thinkers, such as Martin Meredith, by regarding Africa as a continent of hope, at least politically. For example, there are those who would maintain that after many African countries gained independence, the atrocities increased rather than decreased. One example of an opinion that will differ from Benedict's 'hope in Africa' is Martin Meredith, who in his *The Fate of Africa* declared that his book examines "the reasons why, after the euphoria of the independence

---

[127] John Thornton & Susan Varenne, *The Essential Pope Benedict XVI: His central writings & speeches* (New York, HarperCollins: 2007), 335. Cf. *The Rule of St. Benedict*, chapter 72.

era, so many hopes and ambitions faded and why the future of Africa came to be spoken of only in pessimistic terms."[128]

Nevertheless, before evaluating the notion of Africa as a continent of hope, it is worth evaluating the key themes that characterize *Africae Munus,* and that lead to the conclusion that Africa is a continent of hope. It will be made evident, that Benedict's use of hope is not solely sociological but intrinsically embedded within the Christian tradition of Christ our hope – *Christus spes nostra.*

CHRISTOLOGY

Benedict begins his Apostolic Exhortation by clearly pointing out that he is writing to the Universal Church; "in a particular way to the Church in Africa, that she may truly be the 'salt of the earth' and 'light of the world' (cf. *Mt* 5:13-14)."[129] Africa's commitment, together with its neighboring islands, is a commitment to the Lord Jesus Christ. Therefore, to work for reconciliation, justice and peace is to respond to the vocation given by Christ. Africa "is called, in the name of Jesus, to live reconciliation between individuals and communities and to promote peace and justice in truth for all" (1).

The driving force of Africa's commitment is Christ who exhorts Africa to live as brothers and sisters and so promote peace and justice in truth for all. This prerogative is from Christ, the true Prince of Peace. Looking toward Christ, and following his path is to learn the art of peace, of tolerance and of loving even to the point of death. "Only by rejecting people's dehumanization and every compromise prompted by fear of suffering or martyrdom can the cause of the Gospel of truth be served" (30).

---

[128] Martin Meredith, *The Fate of Africa* (New York, Public Affairs Books: 2005), 13-14.
[129] *Africae Munus,* 3.

The sacrifice of Christ on the Cross unites in a deeper way all the Africans who suffer martyrdom for the sake of reconciliation, justice and peace. Tertullian clearly stated: "The blood of martyrs is the seed of the Church". The martyrdom of Africans continues to sustain the faith of the people and leads to a radical conversion to Christ. Conversion to Christ means to have contact with the Word; and by accepting martyrdom, the word of God takes flesh in our lives.

Benedict notes how it is providential that the Synod on the Word of God took place just before the Second Synod for Africa (16). In this sense we can note the relationship between the Word and the Church in Africa. "Through this word, we, the faithful, learn to listen to Christ and to let ourselves be guided by the Holy Spirit, who reveals to us the meaning of all things (cf. *Jn* 16:13)" (16). The *Logos*, who is Christ, is the agent that gives meaning to the pursuit for peace which has to be directed by reconciliation and justice – "the two essential premises of peace..." (16).

ECCLESIOLOGY

Benedict invites the Universal Church to look up to Africa with faith and hope and not fall prey to discouragement. Benedict does not deny the various 'social-political, ethnic, economic, or ecological situations' that Africa faces daily, but emphasizes the depth and richness of the Church's faith where this faith offers hope to the Universal Church. Analogically speaking, the African Church is the spiritual lung of the Church, as Benedict states. "[A] precious treasure is to be found in the soul of Africa, where I perceive a 'spiritual 'lung' for a humanity that appears to be in a crisis of faith and hope'..."[130]

---

[130] *Africae Munus*, 13. Cf. Benedict XVI, *Homily at the Opening Mass of the Second Special Assembly for Africa of the Synod of Bishops* (Vatican City: St. Peter's Basilica, 4 October 2009).

The Church, in Benedict's analysis, should be like Israel, not cast down by discouragement but striving more and more to be a land of promise. "[I]n the face of the many challenges that Africa seeks to address in order to become more and more a land of promise, the Church, like Israel, could easily fall prey to discouragement..."[131] A land of promise is a land where authentic development has taken place – here we also understand why Benedict regards development as not just material but also spiritual, that considers man in his totality – body and soul. In the face of current realities, the Church offers fruits of love: "reconciliation, peace and justice (cf. *Cor* 13:4-7). This is her specific mission" (3).

In addition to calling the Church "Israel", Benedict emphasizes the relevance of calling the Church 'God's family', and of calling Christian families in Africa to become 'domestic churches'. In his *Theology brewed in an African Pot*, Agbonkhianmeghe Orobator mentions how the Church as family is not just a theological utopia. "[I]n the Church called family *all are welcome*. There is a *home* and a place of belonging for everyone in the extended family of God, from which nobody is excluded."[132]

Although Benedict writes particularly to the Church in Africa, he does not stop at a non-existing 'African Ecclesiology,' but connects the Church in Africa with the Ecclesiology of the Universal Church; stating that the Universal Church in the world "will make her specific contribution on the basis of the teaching of the Beatitudes."[133]

The fervent reminder that Benedict makes to the Universal Church is that the image of Christian families as 'domestic churches' "is important not only for the Church in

---

[131] *Africae Munus*, 5.
[132] Agbonkhianmeghe Orobator, *Theology brewed in an African Pot* (New York, Orbis Books: 2008), 89.
[133] *Africae Munus*, 27.

Africa, but also for the universal Church at a time when the family is under threat from those who seek to banish God from our lives" (7), or propose a false anthropology. The Church in service to reconciliation, justice and peace bears testimony to Christ who calls us his brothers and sisters and integrates us into the Trinitarian communion.

SACRAMENTOLOGY

Benedict includes the theology of the Sacraments within this ecclesiological Apostolic Exhortation, particularly the sacraments of Baptism[134] and Penance[135]; in a particular way he accentuated Word and Sacrament as healing remedies.[136] On the other hand, he refers to the Church as Sacrament, most especially when speaking of peace. He states for example: "True peace comes from Christ... It is the peace of a humanity reconciled with itself in God, *a peace of which the Church is the sacrament.*"[137]

The understanding of Church as Sacrament is not new in Catholic theology. Avery Dulles develops the fact that the Church is the sacrament of Christ, because Christ is the sacrament of God.[138] The Second Vatican Council also declared the Church to be a Sacrament, by virtue of the Church's relationship to Christ.[139]

Benedict makes evident that the sacrament of penance is about reconciliation with God, but also reconciliation among people.[140] Therefore, penance in the Church needs to be understood 'vertically' and 'horizontally', i.e., man's reconciliation with God and reconciliation amongst the people.

---

[134] Cf., 32, 41, 131, 162.
[135] Cf., 25, 33, 111, 156.
[136] Cf., 32-38.
[137] Ibid., 30. (My emphasis).
[138] Cf. Avery Dulles, *Models of the Church* (New York, Doubleday & Company, INC.: 1974).
[139] Cf. LG 9, 48; SC 26; GS 42, AG 5.
[140] Cf. *Africae Munus*, 32-34.

From this understanding we can note that sacraments have a 'dialogical structure'. In fact, Avery Dulles pointed out this fact stating that:

> Sacraments therefore have a dialogical structure. They take place in a mutual interaction that permits the people together to achieve a spiritual breakthrough that they could not achieve in isolation. A sacrament therefore is a socially constituted or communal symbol of the presence of grace coming to fulfilment.[141]

In some African traditions, elders have been the chief mediators of reconciliation, and therefore a proper 'inculturation' could be sought so as to find ways towards reconciliation without, nonetheless, banishing the truth of God being the proper giver of forgiveness.[142] Reconciliation, as a goal for Africa is not only to be sought by human endeavors, and particularly by politics. Reconciliation has to find its source in the human heart that is inwardly purified by God. "[U[nless the power of reconciliation is created in people's hearts, political commitment to peace lacks its inner premise" (19).

The sacrament of Baptism, for example, when lived gracefully will allow the members of the Church to be that 'sacrament' of peace that the world needs. Therefore, baptized Christians have to swim against the cultural tide that does not promote justice, peace or reconciliation. Benedict affirms: "[C]hristians are affected by the spirit and customs of their time and place. But by the grace of their Baptism, they are called to reject harmful prevailing currents and to swim against the tide" (32).

---

[141] Avery Dulles, *Models of the Church* (New York, Doubleday & Company, INC.: 1974), 62.
[142] Cf. *Africae Munus*, 33.

The Sacrament of Penance, like Baptism, becomes 'a school of the heart' to which the disciple of Christ "becomes capable of 'confronting the difficulties of social, political, economic and cultural life' through a life permeated with the spirit of the Gospel" (32).

ANTHROPOLOGY

The nature of man as *imago Dei* is central to understanding the human person and his place in society. As St. Irenaeus so eloquently stated: "[F]or by the hands of the Father, that is, by the Son and the Holy Spirit, man, and not [merely] a part of man, was made in the likeness of God."[143]

Benedict notes an 'anthropological crisis', hence the need for Africa to "rediscover and promote a concept of the person and his or her relationship with reality that is the fruit of a profound spiritual renewal."[144] The 'anthropological crisis' causes a culture shock for Africa and hence the inability to confront modernity.

This 'anthropological crisis' is also triggered by the phenomenon of globalization that all people have to confront. Confronting this phenomenon in a Christian way will make the best of society where people will not only view themselves as living side by side but accept each other as brothers and sisters. Hence, contribute to a truly fraternal human family.

The first part of *Africae Munus,* chapter two, is dedicated in fact to the care of the human person in all his dimensions. Within these dimensions, an authentic conversion of heart is what Benedict proposes, while also proposing the reception of the sacrament of penance and experience what reconciliation with God and with others means.[145]

---

[143] Ireneus, *Adversus Haereses* (Grand Rapids, Wm. B. Eerdmans Publishing: 1989), 531.
[144] *Africae Munus*, 11.
[145] Cf. *Africae Munus*, 32-41.

Eschatology

The vision of God is the *telos* of man. As Henri de Lubac noted, "My destiny is something ontological, and not something I can change as anything else changes its destiny."[146] Therefore, to lead man towards development is essentially to lead man to the fullness of development found in the Kingdom of God. "[T]he glory of God is man fully alive,"[147] as Benedict recalls the words of Saint Irenaeus of Lyons. However, the eschatological dimension of Africa to progress can be seen by its radical embrace of Christianity as the exhortation goes: "[A]rise, Church in Africa, Family of God, because you are being called by the heavenly Father!" (148).

What Christ proposes in the pursuit for development so that man may live in accordance with his human dignity is a revolution of love, upon which the Beatitudes are built.[148] As St. Jerome says: "[N]o man is happier than the Christian, for to him is promised the kingdom of heaven."[149] The theological virtues – faith, hope and love – are essential to the Christian life, however only love will be the only virtue needed in heaven, because we shall contemplate him with love as He is Love.[150]

As St. Paul rightly pointed out that the greatest of all virtues is love.[151] This love inspires justice even though it will only be perfected in the Kingdom of God. "[G]od's justice, revealed to us in the Beatitudes, raises the lowly and humbles those who exalt themselves. It will be perfected, it

---

[146] Henri de Lubac. *The Mystery of the Supernatural* (New York, The Crossroads Publishing:1988), 62.
[147] *Africae Munus*, 15.
[148] Cf. Ibid., 26
[149] St. Jerome, *Letters and Select Works* (Grand Rapids, Wm. B. Eerdmans Publishing: 1954), 244.
[150] Cf. Sergio Bonanni, *L'amore che spera e crede* (Roma, Gregorian & Biblical Press: 2010).
[151] Cf. 1 *Cor* 13:13.

is true, in the kingdom of God which is to be fully realized at the end of time. But God's justice is already manifest here and now, wherever the poor are consoled and admitted to the banquet of life."[152]

The eschatological dimension of development is therefore essential not only for Africa but for all people who seek to respond to the vocation of development. Once there is a response to the needs of the poor, and to the concretization of the Works of Mercy, then society lives the 'Already-and-Not-Yet' of the Kingdom of God, a Kingdom of justice and peace. This is the role of the Church, just as "an essential task of the Church is to bring the message of the Gospel to the heart of African societies, to lead people to the vision of God" (15).

PASTORAL THEOLOGY

Evangelization is Christ's work; it is what has caused the faith in Africa to blossom. To evangelize is to be involved in Christ's own ministry of 'pitching a tent amongst his people' – the word of God taking flesh in the lives of people (16). The growing number of Christians in the global South (Africa, Asia, and Latin America) is evidence of the fruits of evangelization; the truth of this claim can be found in Christian demographics, in journals of missiology, and the impacts particularly on culture can be found in Lamin Sanneh's *Translating the Message: The Missionary Impact on Culture*.[153]

Benedict sees the fruits of evangelization as the work of Christ who continues to make Africa the salt of the earth and the light of the world. "In Jesus, some two thousand years ago, God himself brought salt and light to Africa. From that time on, the seed of his presence was buried deep

---

[152] *Africae Munus*, 26.
[153] Cf. Lamin Sanneh, *Translating the Message* (New York, Orbis Books: 2009).

within the hearts of the people of this dear continent, and it has blossomed gradually, beyond and within the vicissitudes of its human history" (11).

The pastoral perspective is central to this Apostolic Exhortation. Benedict, in fact, pronounces, "[H]ence it is with paternal and pastoral concern that I address this document to the Africa of today, which has lived through the traumas and conflicts that we know so well" (11). The Africa of today is also the Africa with a past. This past is marked by traumas and conflicts, as Benedict puts it. It is therefore through *Africae Munus*, that the healing of the past can take effect in order for Africa to progress away from traumas and conflicts. It is interesting to note that Benedict says that he is addressing the document to Africa which has *lived* through traumas and conflicts rather than say that he is addressing the document to Africa which, at least in some countries, *continues to live* through traumas and conflicts.

Evangelization also involves ecumenical and interreligious dialogues, because it is in unity that traumas and conflicts can be eradicated.[154] There are pastoral parameters that the African church needs to consider, and these parameters include working towards development with people of other faiths. "[I]t falls to the particular Churches to translate these parameters into 'resolutions and guidelines for action'" (14).

Benedict is able to recognize the relationship of the Church in Africa with other faiths, because it is through this relationship that a bond of reconciliation can be forged. This might not mean a path to the visible unity of Christians, as the ecumenical goal suggests, but a path to visible unity in the pursuit of reconciliation, justice and peace.

---

[154] Cf. Ibid., 88-96.

AFRICAE MUNUS IN RELATION TO *CARITAS IN VERITATE*

The first connection to be made between the two documents is that: *Africae Munus* is directed to the bishops, priests, consecrated persons and the lay faithful, whereas *Caritas in Veritate* is directed to these but also to all people of good will. Therefore, the audience of the encyclical is the whole world, whereas the audience of the Post-Synodal Apostolic Exhortation is the Christian community. Nevertheless, both documents find their unity in the themes of justice, charity and truth.

In *Africae Munus* Benedict states that: "[J]ustice is never disembodied. It needs to be anchored in consistent human decisions. A charity which fails to respect justice and the rights of all is false."[155] Benedict also makes the same connection between justice and charity in *Caritas in Veritate*. "*Charity goes beyond justice,* because to love is to give, to offer what is 'mine' to the other; but it never lacks justice, which prompts us to give the other what is 'his', what is due to him by reason of his being or his acting."[156]

Another connection to be made is that *Caritas in Veritate* is 'on the integral human development in charity and truth'; whereas *Africae Munus* is 'on the Church in Africa in service to reconciliation, justice and peace', while at the same time concerned with integral human development. However, fraternity, charity and truth are central elements for the pursuit of development and for reconciliation, justice and peace. Both documents seek as well to be involved in the political world because the Church by its nature has a mission of truth to accomplish. "[A]ccording to her social teaching, 'the Church does not have technical solutions to offer and does not claim "to interfere in any way in the politics of states." She does, however, have a mission of truth to ac-

---

[155] *Africae Munus*, 18.
[156] *Caritas in Veritate*, 6.

complish... [one] that the Church can never renounce..."'¹⁵⁷ It should be noted that *Caritas in Veritate* addresses the issue of human development and invites *all persons* to pursue it authentically, through justice, charity and truth. *Africae Munus*, on the other hand, treat of how the *Church in Africa* may serve this development and witness to it. Hence the stress on reconciliation, if justice and peace are to be sought and love prevail.

Indeed, as Benedict eloquently states:

> Human peace obtained without justice is illusory and ephemeral. Human justice which is not the fruit of reconciliation in the 'truth of love' (*Eph* 4:15) remains incomplete; it is not authentic justice. Love of truth – 'the whole truth', to which the Spirit alone can lead us (cf. *Jn* 16:13) – is what marks out the path that all human justice must follow if it is to succeed in restoring the bonds of fraternity within the 'human family, a community of peace', reconciled with God through Christ. (18)

Another point to be noted is that *Africae Munus* in contrast to *Caritas in Veritate* contains many scriptural references, and in addition references from the Catholic patrimony: the Church Fathers, The Catechism of the Catholic Church, the Social Doctrine of the Church and from many other sources such as documents from the Congregation for the Doctrine of the Faith.

The theme of globalization, presented in both documents, cannot be taken lightly for this phenomenon is faced by all people and contributes to development when understood positively. This phenomenon can be understood positively only when it creates a brotherhood of love, based on truth, justice, peace and reconciliation. Globalization is a

---

[157] *Africae Munus*, 22. Cf. *Caritas in Veritate*, 9.

phenomenon that can either be good or bad, as Benedict has noted in *Caritas in Veritate*.[158]

At the same time in *Africae Munus* this theme is also linked to the state of migrants; the Holy Family (Jesus, Mary, and Joseph) are portrayed as the migrants who flee from King Herod and find shelter in Africa (85). In this sense, the phenomenon of globalization and that of migration need particular attention in the area of development, because then the causes of these phenomena can be evaluated and ways that lead to progress can be adopted, for the good of the human person.

AFRICA AND DEVELOPMENT

The theme of development as a vocation is developed in *Populorum Progressio, Caritas in Veritate* and also dealt with in *Africae Munus* - directed specifically to the African continent (24). Justice, peace and reconciliation find their anchor in the central themes already developed in *Caritas in Veritate*; these are the themes of: subsidiarity, solidarity, fraternity, and the like.

Charity is central to development and gives meaning to what 'gift' means – properly speaking gratuitous gift. What Africa can therefore offer is this gift inspired by charity because Africa is capable of contributing to the development of all peoples; this is but a contribution but development is a vocation given to all people. In Benedict's terms:

> Africa is capable of providing every individual and every nation of the continent with the basic conditions which will enable them to share in development. Africans will thus be able to place their God-given talents and riches at the service of their land and their brothers and sisters. If justice is to prevail in all areas of life, private and public, economic and social, it needs to be sustained by

---

[158] Cf. *Africae Munus*, 86, 87. & *Caritas in Veritate*, 36, 42.

subsidiarity and solidarity, and still more, to be inspired by charity.[159]

Development nonetheless cannot exist without God (19). To regard development as a vocation, Paul VI and even Benedict XVI underline the premise of God being the giver of the vocation and man chooses to respond affirmatively or adversely. Nevertheless, not to respond to God's call is not opting for authentic development. This development is not only material but also spiritual as explained earlier that man is composed of body and soul, he needs to develop both materially and spiritually.

The principles of subsidiarity, solidarity and the gift of charity which were thoroughly treated in the analysis of *Caritas in Veritate* emerge again in *Africae Munus*. Firstly, in regard to subsidiarity, Benedict states that: "[I]n accordance with the principle of subsidiarity, neither state nor any larger society should substitute itself for the initiative and responsibility of individuals and intermediary bodies" (24).

Secondly, in regard to solidarity he states: "[S]olidarity is the guarantee of justice and peace, and hence of unity, so that 'the abundance of some compensates for the want of others.'"(24). Finally, in regard to charity, which inspires justice he states that, "[C]harity, which ensures a bond with God, goes beyond distributive justice. For if 'justice is the virtue which assigns to each his due…anything that takes man away from the true God cannot be justice'" (24).

On the sociological plane, very often development is not regarded as a vocation hence as spiritual. This disregard for development as spiritual can be linked to the spiritual crisis that hit the world, particularly the West. On speaking about the reception of the Second Vatican Council, Joseph Ratzinger states an important fact, but what interests us

---

[159] *Africae Munus*, 24.

here is mainly how he confirms the spiritual crisis that hit the Western world. Cardinal Ratzinger states that "the post-conciliar crisis in the Catholic Church coincided with a global spiritual crisis of humanity itself or, at least, of the Western world; not everything that distressed the Church in those years can be attributed to the Council."[160]

Therefore, to work for the true nature of development as a vocation is to work at eradicating the global spiritual crisis of humanity, not only in the Western world, but universally. In this sense, Benedict's engagement with the world is also marked by the recognition of the prevailing spiritual crisis. Therefore, the plea to help Africa to rise, and develop is also a plea to Africa to become the hope of all in the midst of a crisis that seeks to eradicate God from development, and by placing man at the center of development, man becomes the sole agent of his existence.

INCULTURATION

Inculturation has been a theme present in many Papal writings, particularly in John Paul II's *Redemptoris mission,* then again in *Ecclesia in Africa,* and now in Benedict XVI's *Africae Munus.* Post-Colonial Africa does not only wish to develop sociologically but wishes to bring the African soul in all her dimensions: politics, education, finances, and in all that constitutes the African person.

In 1963, Léopald Sédar Senghor, a Catholic, poet, and former president of Senegal, wrote on the subject of inculturation for African priests, insisting on the use of reason and faith. Inculturation needs both reason and faith in order to be a fruitful endeavor, and this can be learned from the

---

[160] Joseph Ratzinger, "Epilogue: On the Status of the Church and Theology Today," *Principles of Catholic Theology: Building Stones for a Fundamental Theology* (San Francisco, Ignatius Press: 1987), 370.

Great African Saint Augustine of Hippo.[161] However, the question that arises for Africa in the *fides et ratio* relationship is the distinction to be made between what constitutes being a Christian in contrast to what is Western. To Christianize Africa is the gift of the Holy Spirit, but to Westernize Africa is to rip people of their identity.[162]

The true agent of inculturation, Benedict notes, is not individuals but the Holy Spirit (37). Benedict does not disregard one of the less developed ecclesiological themes of the Church in Africa, particularly the regard for ancestors. Benedict offers his contribution on how Africa values life and even that of ancestors as the 'living-dead.'[163] This is one of the greatest contributions that Benedict can offer to a Church that is still in search of an 'authentic local theology' that considers culture while not disregarding the Christian culture (69).[164]

To be involved in the process of inculturation is to bring together the Christian culture in rapport with the local culture. In this case, Christianity and African culture/cultures in the African Continent. Nevertheless, this process cannot be understood as one culture entering another but a reciprocal relationship where discernment, purification and decision-making take place. To be able to harmoniously 'inculturate' will mean reaching a point of authentic integration.

When we place the thoughts of Benedict on inculturation in relation to his thoughts on development presented in *Caritas in Veritate*, we ought to conclude that inculturation is not solely an ecclesial matter, but ought to even take place

---

[161] Joseph Roger de Benoist, *Léopold Sédar Senghor* (Paris, Beauchesne: 1998), 211. "*Que tous les Africains prennent exemple sur saint Augustin, le Grand Africain, qui avait parfaitement élucidé le problem. Ce don't il s'agit, ce n'est pas d'opposer le ratio et la foi, la raison discursive et la raison intuitive, la Loi et l'Amour; c'est de les unir dans une symbiose fervente – en avant.*"
[162] Cf. *Africae Munus*, 168.
[163] *Africae Munus*, 173.
[164] Cf. Michael Paul Gallagher, *Clashing Symbols* (Darton, Longman & Todd: 2003).

in governmental structures. For example, when speaking of the sacrament of Penance, Benedict recommends the role that elders play in reconciliation. In like manner, the elders can be recommended in their role of local governance, because "[t]raditional chiefs have a very positive contribution to make in good governance."[165]

What seem to be missing in Benedict's view on traditional chiefs are the changes that have occurred after colonization. Traditional chiefs before colonization had a role which after colonization changed considerably. Martin Meredith, for example, notes this considerable change.

> In much of Africa, therefore, the colonial imprint was barely noticeable... In many cases, however, African chiefs came to constitute no more than a new class of intermediaries paid to transmit government orders. As agents of colonial rule, the role they played was far removed from their traditional position at the apex of authority, balancing many diverse interests. Some chiefs were members of old royal families carefully selected for their willingness to collaborate; others had no traditional legitimacy at all. The *chefs de canton* appointed by the French were effectively administrative officers chosen from the ranks of the more efficient clerks and interpreters in government services. In some cases where chiefs did not exist, as among the acephalous village societies of the Igbo of southern Nigeria, chiefdoms were invented. In other cases, "traditional" chiefs were left bereft of all functions.[166]

These issues about chiefs should be considered; something which does not seem to feature in Benedict's proposal to incorporate chiefs in matters of reconciliation. One error that could be made when speaking about Africa is to place all

---

[165] *Africae Munus*, 81.
[166] Martin Meredith, *The Fate of Africa* (New York, Public Affairs Books: 2005), 5-6.

African issues into one category as if Africa is not a continent but one single village. However, as there are different cultures in the West, so are there in Africa. The Germans in Europe for example, are different from the Italians; in like manner, the South Africans are different from the Nigerians. So, to what extent one can speak of Africa and not particular African contexts is not an easy analysis to make.

In this line of thought, it is important to stress that Christianity is not a European religion as some would wrongly affirm. Cardinal Joseph Ratzinger, in his talk *Europe's Crisis of Culture* given in Subiaco, Italy on the 1st April 2005, explained the development of Christianity in a way that one could understand the European influence that Christianity received. "[C]hristianity, it is true, did not start in Europe, and therefore it cannot even be classified as a European religion, the religion of the European cultural realm. But it received precisely in Europe its most effective cultural and intellectual imprint and remains, therefore, identified in a special way with Europe."[167]

We could therefore conclude that, as Christianity grows in Africa, it finds itself in confrontation with traditions that never knew of Christianity. Inculturation will then mean that Christianity will receive an effective 'African cultural and intellectual imprint', for years to come. This imprint will also invigorate the Universal Church, especially due to the phenomenon of globalization. This imprint will also positively carry Christianity to be truly universal - for all peoples. In a way, like Benedict we can say that "Christianity will thus adopt the face of the countless cultures and peoples among whom it has found a welcome and taken root. The Church will then become an icon of the future

---

[167] John Thornton & Susan Varenne, *The Essential Pope Benedict XVI: His central writings & speeches* (New York, HarperCollins: 2007), 327.

which the Spirit of God is preparing for us, an icon to which Africa has a contribution of her own to make."[168]

AFRICAN STORIES OF FRATERNITY

African stories have shifted from being stories of gloom as depicted by the Roman Pliny the Elder, to being stories of hope by Benedict XVI. As former President of the Republic of South Africa, Thabo Mbeki noted at his talk to the United Nations University (9 April 1998) speaking of the African renaissance, that Africa is a nation of hope.

The shift made is from stories that have been read mainly by a non-African audience that only speak of savagery and doom. Pliny the Elder, for example, depicted Africa thus:

> Of the Ethiopians there are diverse forms and kinds of men. Some there are toward the east that have neither nose nor nostrils, but the face all full. Others that have no upper lip, they are without tongues, and they speak by signs, and they have but a little hole to take their breath at, by which they drink with an oaten straw ... In a part of Afrikke be people called Pteomphane, for their King they have a dog, at whose fancy they are governed ... And the people called Anthropomphagi which we call cannibals, live with human flesh. The Cinamolgi, their heads are almost like to heads of dogs... Blemmyis a people so called, they have no heads, but hide their mouth and their eyes in their breasts.[169]

These stories are gloomy, and as Thabo Mbeki noted: "'[t]hese images must have frightened many a Roman child to scurry to bed whenever their parents said, "The Africans

---

[168] *Africae Munus*, 37.
[169] Thabo Mbeki, The *African Renaissance, South Africa and the World* (Talk given at United Nations University: 9 April 1998).

are coming! The strange creatures out of Africa are coming!'" (Mbeki).

The shift has been made in the writings of missionaries and many competent Africans such as Emmanuel Katongole. In his book *The Sacrifice of Africa*, Emmanuel Katongole argues that stories are essential to Africa. "[S]ocial ethics in Africa need to focus more on stories than on skills. Such a focus not only offers tremendous opportunities for Christianity, but also provides a fresh appreciation of how all politics is grounded in stories..."[170]

These are stories of how people live and what they experience on a day-to-day basis. At first it might seem as though Katongole is talking about fictional tales that are popular to African literature, such as the tales of Chinua Achebe in his novels. Nonetheless, the tales told by Achebe such as in *Things fall Apart* contain an important message on how to confront tribalism, death and acceptance.

Traditional African elders have often transmitted life lessons to the young in the form of parables, and the young have been shaped by these life lessons. In fact, Benedict also states how the elderly, including traditional leaders, have an important role to play in development through transmitting wisdom. "[I]t is because of this wisdom, sometimes obtained at a high price, that the elderly can influence the family in a variety of ways. Their experience naturally leads them not only to bridge the generation gap, but also to affirm the need for mutual support."[171]

The stories that shape the human development of the African child are those about food and hunger, about peace in the midst of violence, poverty, segregation, as well as stories about hope and conquest, comparable with the liberation of the Israelites from Egypt the land of slavery.

---

[170] Emmanuel Katongole, *The Sacrifice of Africa* (Michigan, Grand Rapids: 2011), 21.
[171] *Africae Munus*, 47.

They are the stories shaped by scripture; "the biblical stories and the contemporary stories illuminate each other in a way that both reveals the limits of nation-state politics in Africa and provides an interruption and alternative to it." [172] However, what Katongole fails to clearly state is that these stories are about brotherhood – the very notion of *Ubuntu*.

THE CHURCH AD EXTRA

The African stories shape the politics and the faith of the African people. They are the stories lived by Christian men and women and non-Christians alike. They are the stories of Rwandans killed because of the tribe they are born into. Stories of how the world nations remain silent to the plea of the helpless. They are stories of lies, where Christians call each other brothers and sisters and yet refuse to extend a helping hand to a brother or sister in need. Confronting these stories and not denying their existence is to confront the truth that comes from God – Eternal Love and Absolute Truth.[173]

To deny the existence of injustices, poverty, hunger, wars, unequal distribution of wealth, and bad governance is not the truth. At the same time, to fail to be Eucharistic people is a lie. Maggy Barankitse, the foundress of the *Maison Shalom* in Burundi says the Eucharist is 'us' (Katongole, 187). The Eucharist is Jesus and he is also the *Veritas par excellence*. For a Christian to deny the truth is to deny Jesus and hence to embrace a false religion not based on love. Maggy is one woman, who will "contribute to the humanization of society,"[174] to use the words of Benedict.

The Church as an institution responds to social needs and not just intra-ecclesial issues because of the call to love; a call felt by all people. This extra-ecclesial concern for

---

[172] Emmanuel Katongole, *The Sacrifice of Africa* (Michigan, Grand Rapids: 2011), 25.
[173] *Caritas in Veritate*, 1.
[174] *Africae Munus*, 57.

others has an ecumenical dimension because irrespective of religion, all people are children of God and constitute the common brotherhood of all.

Social problems are not problems of the State but are problems for all people to confront. When one is in hunger, the whole world is affected, not just the individual, because that one person belongs to the collective human race and is therefore never alone. Angelina, the co-foundress of Concerned Parents Association, makes this notion clear by saying "all these children are mine" (Katongole, 161). When the rebels in Uganda kidnapped children and made a deal with her to release her daughter in exchange of her silence about the rebel dealings in Uganda, she refused. She understood the basic value of *fraternitas*; above all she understood what it means to embrace the notions of transparency, honesty, and responsibility.[175]

All these stories of hope offer something new not just for Africa but for the whole world, because Africa is a continent of hope. With great certitude then we can say that *ex Africa semper aliquid novi* (something new always comes out of Africa).

THE CHURCH AS A FAMILY AND A FRATERNITY

Africae Munus 8, recalling *Ecclesia in Africa* 8 reaffirms the Church as a family and a fraternity. This image of Church as family "emphasizes care for others, solidarity, warmth in human relationships, acceptance, dialogue, and trust."[176] In Benedict's analysis the family is also "the 'sanctuary of life' and a vital cell of society and of the Church" (42).

It is in *Africae Munus* 18, that Benedict exhorts Christians directly to be exemplary in practicing justice and charity.

---

[175] Cf. *Caritas in Veritate*, 36.
[176] *Africae Munus*, 7.

"[I] therefore encourage Christians to become exemplary in the area of justice and charity (*Mt* 5:19-20)" (18). This kind of encouragement is not found in *Caritas in Veritate* where Benedict exhorts the whole of humanity to practice charity and truth, whereas here the call is for the Christian community to be exemplary to the whole world.

The "moving testimonies of the faithful on suffering", have helped the Church to re-establish fraternity as Benedict states (20). The sharing of the sufferings of the people have been a platform of re-establishing a fraternity. This is what it means to be brothers and sisters to one another – to suffer with the other, to aid the other in the time of need. This is what a Christian family does – be concerned for the other.

Africae Munus offers solutions that were not as explicit in *Caritas in Veritate* on the importance of the family in creating fraternity and working towards justice and peace and human development (43). What Benedict offers is a new understanding of development, which might be called moral development. As he states:

> The problem of AIDS, in particular, clearly calls for a medical and pharmaceutical response. This is not enough, however: the problem goes deeper. Above all, it is an ethical problem. The change of behavior that it requires – for example, sexual abstinence, rejection of sexual promiscuity, fidelity within marriage – ultimately involves the question of integral development, which demands a global approach and a global response from the Church.

What becomes a crisis for Africa regarding marriage in the modern world, are the goods which the African Saint Augustine of Hippo upheld with great vigor. St. Augustine mentioned the three goods of marriage being: "offspring (*proles*), mutual fidelity (*fides*), and the sacramental bond (*sacramentum*)."[177] These three goods find themselves as 'choices' rather than 'goods'; this is much more present in North America and Europe; hence Benedict sees Africa as the light of the world, and salt of the earth that can remind the rest of the world of these important components of human life.

A NEW BROTHERHOOD

In Christ all is made new, a brotherhood that has boundaries is transformed to be an open brotherhood where all shall be united. "Through Christ, their one model, the just are invited to enter the order of love – *agape*."[178] It is noteworthy that by practicing the Corporal Works of Mercy, the Church tries to forge a new Africa – this new Africa cannot be anything but a new brotherhood where love is central. "Through her ability to see the face of Christ on the face of children, the sick, the needy and those who suffer, the Church is helping slowly but surely to forge a new Africa" (30).

The theme of fraternity is important for Africa, for from being a 'marginalized' continent, like the disregarded brother, Africa is once again incorporated into the human fraternity. It is through Christian Africa that the true meaning of brotherhood is adopted over the political slogans such as comrade or compatriot. Realities such as slave trade and colonization are what led to the 'marginalization' of Africa, even though "[t]oday too, the continent has to cope with rivalries and with new forms of enslavement and colonization" (9).

Benedict is explicit about the theme of the Eucharist, whereas he is not in *Caritas in Veritate*. He states how the Eucharist and the Scriptures are the forces that create a

---

[177] Augustine. *De bono conjugali (The Excellence of marriage)* (Hyde Park, New City Press: 1999), 30.
[178] *Africae Munus*, 25.

fraternity and place us at the service of others (41). In a sense we could say that 'we become what we receive.' The Eucharist is what we receive and so we, therefore, also become Eucharistic people. Transubstantiation as such is not only about the transformation of the elements of bread and wine, as we can note in the Eucharistic prayer of St. Basil, but is also the transformation of the Christian community. It is in receiving Him that we become like Him; it is in listening to His word that we can be that 'unspoken word' to others for by our deeds we bear testimony to his word.

PRINCIPAL PARAMETERS OF MISSION

The pastoral concerns and proposals that Benedict offers in *Africae Munus* derive from all the documentation of the Second Synodal Assembly, and these documents call for "transforming theology into pastoral care, namely into a very concrete pastoral ministry in which the great perspectives found in sacred Scripture and Tradition find application in the activity of bishops and priests in specific times and places."[179]

The pastoral solutions that Benedict proposes are what will maintain the Christian *joie de vivre*. As he states, for example, in the midst of great pandemics such as malaria, AIDS, and tuberculosis, "[A]frica maintains its *joie de vivre*, celebrating God's gift of life by welcoming children for the increase of the family circle and the human community" (9).

One observes that there is a comparison between Africa and other continents where for example, there are no great pandemics, but the fact of not welcoming children, engaging in abortion, euthanasia and the like, is itself a form of a "great pandemic." What Benedict proposes is therefore maintaining the *joie de vivre* in Jesus who remains the only physician to heal us.

---

[179] *Africae Munus*, 10.

Chapter Five

Critical Comments on the Encyclical

FRATERNITAS AT THE CORE OF THE ENCYCLICAL

Caritas in Veritate, written to address current economic, social and political issues, as a follow-up to the encyclical of Paul VI *Populorum Progressio*, responds to these issues especially in the interest of the poor. It is in the interest of the poor that Benedict develops an understanding of fraternity that may be accepted by all people, and not only by Catholics or other Christians. The understanding of fraternity therefore takes on concrete expression and is not simply the application of an abstract notion. Since the encyclical is directed to all peoples, Pope Benedict appeals primarily to the workings of reason, though reason enlightened by faith, and the specific reality of fellowship and communion as lived among Christians is secondary, pertaining to the witness that Christians are to give to the world in the name of Jesus Christ.

Having written of the issues to be developed, the encyclical dedicates the third chapter to the theme of 'Fraternity, Economic Development and Civil Society', and throughout links it to the principle of gratuitousness as key to the hope of civilizing the economy. Looking for a fuller, more expressly theological presentation of brotherhood, one may turn to the theological writings of Joseph Ratzinger, particularly *The Meaning of Christian Brotherhood*, as a *crux interpretationis* of *Caritas in Veritate*.

The encyclical, even though not only directed to Christians, can be understood by returning to the other sources such as the Social Doctrine of the Church, Joseph Ratzinger's early literature, and of a more pastoral dimension *Africae Munus*. It is in these sources that somehow show the development made in *Caritas in Veritate* that one grasps the centrality of Christology, and the meaning of fraternity as presented in the encyclical.

The concerns raised in the encyclical, parallel those mentioned in *Africae Munus,* as observed by Lisa Cahill in her article *Caritas in Veritate: Benedict's Global Reorientation.*[180]

One of the critical comments that can be made about the encyclical is that by being Christologically and Ecclesiologically centered it calls all people to understand the language used, therefore a return to theological sources. In fact, Benedict states: "[I]t is one thing to draw attention to the particular characteristics of one Encyclical or another, of the teaching of one Pope or another, but quite another to lose sight of the coherence of the overall doctrinal *corpus.*"[181] Benedict says this specifically in reference to *Populorum Progressio,* which he wants to place within the context of the *corpus* of the Church's social teaching.

THE DIFFICULTY OF THE TEXT

Caritas in Veritate is not an easy read. For one, there is the difficulty of understanding the language. Drew Christiansen S.J., although understanding the text very well, finds it too difficult to be comprehended when expounded in lofty terms. The understanding of the text calls us back to Cardinal Peter Turkson's story already narrated about Rossana in the slums of Kenya.[182] Turkson, as he tells the story which he himself received from Fr. Michael Czerney S.J. states how Rossana could grasp the realities of the encyclical, saying that the text of Pope Benedict refers to her slum,

---

[180] Cf. Lisa Cahill, *Caritas in Veritate: Benedict's Global Reorientation* (Theological studies, June 2010; 71, 2).
[181] *Caritas in Veritate,* 12.
[182] Cardinal Peter K.A. Turkson, *Caritas in Veritate: Good News for Society* (Article from Logos: A Journal of Catholic Thought and Culture, Volume 15, Number 3, Summer 2012), 90-108.

where the rich subdue the poor; she also coins the term 'global slum.'[183] How much she understands the rest of the encyclical is not clear. So, as Christiansen notes, first there is the difficulty of the text.[184]

The points raised and treated by Christiansen are firstly, the range of issues addressed and the difficulty of finding a vocabulary for current social, economic and political realities. Secondly, the encyclical's effort to relate its teachings to the entire documentary tradition of Catholic social teaching. Thirdly, the swing between abstract concepts and concrete applications. Fourthly, the presentation of a metaphysical foundation, which is rooted in a European philosophical tradition, and which is strongly influenced in this case by St. Augustine's Neo-Platonism, and lastly, the constant appeal to relativism in speaking of current culture and thought as expressed in *Caritas in Veritate*.

Since the text speaks much about how the rich subdue the poor, the text does not seem to cater, at least linguistically, to the poor who mostly are afflicted by poverty and illiteracy.[185] The text needs a 'retranslation' into a simpler language that the poor may understand, and not just the educated. The encyclical needs to be translated into local languages or dialects of the very poor (especially in countries of the South), and this can be said for many other papal writings, including *Africae Munus* directed to Africa which as a continent has the highest rate of illiteracy compared to other continents.

---

[183] Ibid., "I know the encyclical is about the whole world, but when I read the Pope's words, he is talking exactly about Kenya, even my slum. He says that the market must not become 'the place where the strong subdue the weak,' but it is. Billions of us live as neighbors to one another in our global village – or is it a global slum? – yet with too little fraternal relationship."

[184] Drew Christiansen, *Metaphysics and Society: A Commentary on Caritas in Veritate* (Theological studies, June 2010; 71, 2), 26ff.

[185] Cf. *Caritas in Veritate*, 21.

One other criticism that comes from the difficulty of the text is how it could be translated into everyday life. There have been a considerable number of articles on the translation of the encyclical for better understanding. One worth mentioning is written by Amelia Uelman, published in *Theological Studies;* this article in particular links the encyclical to Chiara Lubich' spirituality of unity.[186] However, more articles that link the encyclical to other areas such as spirituality, justice and peace, philosophy, economics, bioethics, and the like, are needed so that integral human development does not remain the pursuit of a few but of all people working together as brothers and sisters.

CARITAS IN VERITATE IN RELATION TO AFRICA

Orobator in his article *Caritas in Veritate and Africa's Burden of (under)Development* wonders whether Benedict had in mind anything other than European Catholicism, because he does not mention Africa by name. "Reading Pope Benedict XVI's encyclical *Caritas in Veritate* (2009) on integral human development elicits wonder about whether the pope had anything in mind other than European Catholicism."[187] This is why it has been helpful to see the application of social teaching and the understanding of *fraternitas* in relation to *Africae Munus.*

Without wanting to misrepresent Orobator on whether *Caritas in Veritate* does or does not address global issues too narrowly from a viewpoint of 'European Catholicism', without taking non-European developments into account, it is important to state some facts. Firstly, the encyclical is directed to the Universal Church but also to all people of good will. Secondly, the encyclical was written in connection with

---

[186] Amelia J. Uelman, *Caritas in Veritate and Chiara Lubich* (Theological Studies, June 2010; 71, 2).
[187] Agbonkhianmeghe Orobator, *Caritas in Veritate and Africa's Burden of (Under)Development* (Theological Studies, June 2010; 71, 2), 320.

the global economic and financial crisis which not only affected North America and European countries alone, but also many other countries of the South, because of the relationships in trade, market and subsidies received from the more affected countries. Lastly, since the encyclical is on integral human development, what the pope has in mind is humanity as a whole, and this is what his predecessors had in mind as well, e.g., Paul VI and John Paul II.

Benedict is not a conceptualist but a realist in the area of development. He is able to discern what society needs today in order to build a better future for humanity. The crisis of underdevelopment (material and spiritual) is what drives Benedict to realistically state what could be done in order to achieve human development and shape a new vision for the future.

> The different aspects of the crisis, its solutions, and any new development that the future may bring, are increasingly interconnected, they imply one another, they require new efforts of holistic understanding and a *new humanistic synthesis*. The complexity and gravity of the present economic situation rightly cause us concern, but we must adopt a realistic attitude as we take up with confidence and hope the new responsibilities to which we are called by the prospect of a world in need of profound cultural renewal, a world that needs to rediscover fundamental values on which to build a better future.[188]

Throughout the encyclical, Benedict argues for a true humanism anchored on Christ; this humanism considers man in his totality – body and soul. Benedict does not define development as solely material, as Orobator tries to suggest by focusing solely on 'material poverty', but development is both spiritual and material – it embodies the whole of man.

---

[188] *Caritas in Veritate*, 21.

"Development must include not just material growth but also *spiritual growth*, since the human person is a 'unity of body and soul', born of God's creative love and destined for eternal life."[189] Holistic development and the pursuit for the common good, has to consider the whole of man. Africa in a sense offers the spiritual growth that the Western countries, for example, can adopt.

It is true that *Caritas in Veritate* is a dense text and one needs to analyze the text with great patience, but it would be incorrect to focus Benedict's encyclical on the understanding of development as only material and not spiritual. Development, as a vocation is not void of the spiritual dimension.

When we consider the richness of Africa's faith, for example, we should also consider the European imprint that this Continent has received. Although as Ratzinger, Benedict saw the European Christian imprint as important for Christianity, it seems that in *Africae Munus*, he exhorts Africa to offer purification to this imprint. Europe has lost some of the important imprints, but most of Africa has not lost these but seeks to enculturate them in the local Churches.

Orobator offers a number of criticisms on the encyclical, which range from the relationship between the encyclical and Africa, to the status of women, to justice and the Church (*ad extra et ad intra*). Although Orobator understands Paul VI's and Benedict's consideration of development as a vocation, he does not emphasize the integral dimension of development as both material and spiritual. Orobator states, for example: "[A]dditional measures are needed if the justice, solidarity, and equity that *Caritas in Veritate* promotes as vital ingredients of development are to become available for women as well as for men. Presently, in church more

---

[189] Ibid., 76. (Italics in the original).

than in society, this message needs a clearer and more honest articulation" (Orobator, 330-331).

One of the strongest criticisms that Orobator makes is on the issue of justice within the Church, or as he prefers to call it 'domestic justice'. In a way, we might say the common expression, 'charity begins at home', is transformed by Orobator's criticism as 'justice begins at home'. For Orobator, Benedict focuses on the need for justice in society but does not focus on the need for justice within the Church. This criticism is worth exploring. Firstly, Orobator poses a question: "[I]n the context of *Caritas in Veritate* the question arises: if development is as integral as Benedict correctly claims it is, at what point does the axis of flaws, ills, and failings of secular and global social, political, and economic realms intersect with that of the community called 'church'?" (Orobator, 329-330).

After posing this question, Orobator supports his claim by quoting the 1971 Synod of Bishop's document *Justitia in mundo*, which in essence spoke of the Church being an example of justice in the eyes of people.[190] Orobator continues:

> Cultural or traditional attitudes that impede integral human development do not reside exclusively within the secular realm; 'modes of acting' inimical to integral development can be 'found within the Church herself.' Thus, principles and criteria by which *Caritas in Veritate* criticizes and excoriates social, political, and economic systems could prove useful and apt in evaluating the openness of the community called 'church,' for example, in the exercise of authority, equality in mission, and attentiveness to the needs of the marginalized, impoverished, and vulnerable. (Orobator, 329-330)

---

[190] *Justitia in Mundo*, 40.

As Benedict stated about reading the encyclical in relation to other sources of the Church's patrimony, it seems in this regard that Orobator, posing the criticism on 'domestic justice', focusses on the encyclical itself while not returning to the Church's teachings on topics about the exercise of authority, and the like.

The criticism posed is influenced by a sociological need to 'empower' the so called 'marginalized', while paying no heed to Church patrimony which is not just materially centered, so to speak, but also spiritually informed.

What Orobator's criticism lacks is the understanding of 'rights' and 'duties' in both society and the Church; "it is important to call for a renewed reflection on how *rights presuppose duties, if they are not to become mere licence.*"[191]

Benedict, influenced by St. Augustine of Hippo, did already give a warning to this kind of understanding held by Orobator: "The *earthly city*", Benedict stated, "is promoted not merely by relationships of rights and duties, but to an even greater and more fundamental extent by relationships of gratuitousness, mercy and communion" (6). The Church speaks of justice because justice is already present as a gift within the Church of Christ. Where there are elements of a lack of justice, it is the Church herself that is reminded of her own teaching of the importance of transparency, honesty, truth, charity and fraternity.

In the light of all these observations made, the pursuit is for *Caritas in Veritate,* but it is always Christ's charity that urges us on – *Caritas Christi urget nos*. It is this charity that also urges us to create authentic fraternal bonds, in charity and truth.[192]

---

[191] *Caritas in Veritate*, 43.
[192] Cf. Ibid., 20.

THE RELATIONSHIP BETWEEN CHURCH AND STATE

The teaching of Joseph Ratzinger, continued later as Pope, is centered on Christology and Ecclesiology. Through his teachings on the relationship between faith and reason, he makes evident the relationship between Church and state. Within this relationship it is clear that the Church does not seek to divinize the state but to help it to respond in charity and truth to the development of all peoples. Both Church and state are called to act according to their own essence and not try to merge. In his *Values in a time of upheaval*, Ratzinger notes:

> The Church remains something 'outside' the state, for only thus can both Church and state be what they are meant to be. Like the state, the Church too must remain in its proper place and within its boundaries. It must respect its own being and its own freedom, precisely in order to be able to perform for the state the service that the latter requires. The Church must exert itself with all its vigor so that in it there may shine forth the moral truth that it offers to the state and that ought to become evident to the citizens of the state. This truth must be vigorous within the Church, and it must form men, for only then it will have the power to convince others and to be a force working like a leaven for all of society.[193]

On the topic of development, there is a need for both Church and state to work together. However, it is noticeable in *Caritas in Veritate*, that Benedict focusing on the theme of fraternity breaks the boundaries of any state, people or culture. *Caritas in Veritate* does not seem to adopt a strict relationship between church and state but embraces a much larger global reality, with its economic, social and political organization.

---

[193] Joseph Ratzinger, *Values in a Time of Upheaval* (San Francisco, Ignatius Press: 2006), 69-70.

Development, as has already been mentioned, is not only material but is also spiritual, hence a vocation. Benedict's global reorientation it could be said is based on the relationship he traces out between faith and reason, Church and state.

Reason, however, does not, in Benedict's global reorientation, take the place of mere concepts but it is the Logos of God – 'creative reason'. By accepting reason as the Logos of God, this purifies the understanding of development to be viewed firstly as a vocation and therefore as both material and spiritual.

Cahill, mentions that in order to understand the theology of Pope Benedict, it is important to read his books on *Jesus of Nazareth* (Joseph Ratzinger/Pope Benedict XVI). Cahill also correctly relates how the Person of Jesus (Human and Divine) is at the center of Benedict's writings, principally traced out in *Deus caritas est* and then in *Caritas in Veritate*.

> Benedict's theology, centered on a relation to God in Christ, aims to bolster the countercultural voice of the Catholic Church against modernizing trends in European culture. This theology is most fully displayed in Benedict's book *Jesus of Nazareth,* and backs his first encyclical, *Deus caritas est. Caritas in Veritate,* however, is a concrete response to global poverty and violence, especially the inequities and imbalances of power that lie behind the global economic crisis of 2008 to 2010. The context and politics of *Caritas in Veritate* demand a Christology with a robust connection among the divine, the human, and social change.[194]

Caritas in Veritate reopens dialogue between Church and state, with the hope of working together towards human

---

[194] Lisa Cahill, *Caritas in Veritate: Benedict's Global Reorientation* (Theological Studies, June 2010; 71, 2), 291.

development in charity and truth. Nevertheless, the encyclical alone cannot be taken as a working text, it is the primary text of course, but secondary sources are necessary in order to delve into the underlying issues that led to the publication of this encyclical. At the same time, the state and its way of governance has to be understood from historical data to its present position. Issues of independence from colonial rule cannot be ignored; the phenomenon of globalization too cannot be ignored. In a nutshell, all historical and current social issues cannot be ignored because that is what affects the human person living in society.

In *Church, Ecumenism, and Politics*, Ratzinger called the state a *societas imperfecta*. "[T]he state remains the *societas imperfecta* and that it still calls now for another entity that is capable of completing it and revealing to it the moral forces that it cannot draw up from its own depths."[195] The Church, therefore as the *societas perfecta* is the only entity that is capable of completing and revealing moral forces to the state. People like Jean-Jacques Rousseau would never agree with Benedict on this point, since for Rousseau the Church, like absolute monarchy, is a cause of corruption that enslaves people.[196]

Benedict would say that before we classify ourselves as citizens of a particular country, we are firstly children of God and citizens of heaven towards which we are directed. Therefore, there should be a 'productive-functional relationship' between Church and state. "[W]here the church itself becomes the state, freedom is gone. But freedom is lacking also in places where the church is abolished as a public and publicly relevant authority, because there again the

---

[195] Joseph Ratzinger, *Church, Ecumenism, and Politics* (San Francisco, Ignatius Press: 2008), 202.
[196] Cf. Jean-Jacques Rousseau, *On the Social Contract* (Indianapolis, Hackett Publishing Company: 1987).

state claims to be the sole basis for morality."[197] The question of citizenship is a serious question for humanity. Being Christian should be the first and most important affiliation before being affiliated to the *civitas terrena*.[198]

The truth for Benedict as evidenced in *Caritas in Veritate*, is found in Christ, who is the *Veritas* itself. Leo XIII, Paul VI, John Paul II, Pope Benedict XVI and many other moral voices, would say that the truth is the way to true development and authentic liberation, and that the Church bears witness to the truth. In order to live as brothers and sisters and strive for authentic development, charity and truth are vital.

---

[197] Ibid., p. 157.
[198] Ratzinger, *Church, Ecumenism, and Politics* (San Francisco, Ignatius Press: 2008), 201. "The *civitas Dei* [city of God] cannot become an empirical political entity…in this sense it remains nonempirical. For its part, the state in every case can only be a *civitas terrena* [an earthly city]."

Conclusion

This book has presented an analysis of the notion of fraternity as developed in the encyclical *Caritas in Veritate*. At the same time, this same notion has been related to the context of the African Church, considering Benedict XVI's post-synodal-exhortation *Africae Munus*.

In his encyclical, Pope Benedict exhorts the world to be serious about human development. Like the clown, related in Kierkegaard's story in the first chapter, we can also affirm that *Caritas in Veritate* calls us to be serious about the fire of underdevelopment consuming society – this is no illusion but calls for a response.

Benedict's point of departure is Christological, as has been demonstrated. His Christology, however in *Caritas in Veritate,* considers all people of good will, whereas in *Africae Munus* considers the Catholic community. It has been the scope of this book that the notion of fraternity in its transcendental and Christological references, as presented in *Caritas in Veritate,* will shape an authentic humanism where people live as brothers and sisters to one another. Due to the phenomenon of globalization, more and more people live as mere neighbors, side by side. But fraternity demands love, truth and tolerance to which Christ, and in turn, the Church, are the divinely given witness.

While working on this book, Pope Benedict XVI made it public that he would resign as Supreme Pontiff on the 28th February 2013, on the feast of Our Lady of Lourdes (11 February 2013). After his resignation, Pope Francis was chosen in conclave and now occupies the Chair of St. Peter. In his opening words as pope, Francis spoke of the need to pray for the great spirit of fraternity to exist in the world.

In conclusion, it is fitting to end with the very words of Pope Francis, "And now, we take up this journey: Bishop and People. This journey of the Church of Rome which presides in charity over all the Churches. A journey of fraternity, of love, of trust among us. Let us always pray for one another. Let us pray for the whole world, that there may be a great spirit of fraternity."[199]

With these words, Pope Francis shows us the continuing work that needs to be done in relating fraternity, charity, and truth to the on-going development of a global humanity. It is hopeful that more research be done in relating the theme of fraternity to the whole *corpus* of Catholic social teaching.

---

[199] Pope Francis, Apostolic Blessing – *Urbi et Orbi* (13 March 2013, Vatican City).

Bibliography

Primary Texts

Benedict XVI. *Caritas in Veritate*. Vatican City: Libreria Editrice Vaticana, 2009.

Benedict XVI. *Deus Caritas est*. Vatican City: Libreria Editrice Vaticana, 2005.

Benedict XVI. *Spe Salvi*. Vatican City: Libreria Editrice Vaticana, 2007.

John Paul II. *Centesimus Annus*. Vatican City: Libreria Editrice Vaticana, 1991.

Paul VI. *Populorum Progressio*. Vatican City: Libreria Editrice Vaticana, 1967.

Pius XI. *Quadragesimo Anno*. Vatican City: Libreria Editrice Vaticana, 1931.

Pope Benedict XVI. *Africae Munus*. Vatican City: Libreria Editrice Vaticana, 2011.

Secondary Texts:

Augustine, (R.W. Dyson ed.) *The City of God against the Pagans*. Cambridge: Cambridge University Press, 2002.

Augustine. *De bono conjugali (The Excellence of marriage)*. Hyde Park: New City Press, 1999.

Augustine. *The City of God*. Translated by Marcus Dods. New York: Random House, 1978.

Blessed C. Marmion, (Alan Bancroft trans.) *Christ, The Life of the Soul*. Herefordshire: Gracewing Publishing, 2005.

Bonanni, Sergio. *L'amore che spera e crede*. Roma: Gregorian & Biblical Press, 2010.

Catechism of the Catholic Church. Nairobi: Paulines Publications Africa, 2002.

Cavanaugh, William T. *Migrations of the Holy: God, State, and the Political Meaning of the Church*. Grand Rapids: Eerdmans Publishing Co., 2011.

Christiansen, Drew. "Metaphysics and Society: A Commentary on *Caritas in Veritate*." *Theological Studies*, June 2010; 71, 2.

Christiansen, Drew. "Metaphysics and Society: A Commentary on *Caritas in Veritate*." *Theological Studies* 71 (2010), 3-4.

Chu Ilo, Stan. *The Church and development in Africa*. Oregon: Pickwick Publications, 2011.
De Lubac, Henri. *Catholicism*. Translated by Lancelot C. Sheppard and Elizabeth Englund. San Francisco: Ignatius Press, 1988.
De Lubac, Henri. *A Brief Catechesis on Nature and Grace*. Translated by Richard Arnandez. San Francisco: Ignatius Press, 1980.
De Lubac, Henri. *At the Service of the Church*, trans. Anne Elizabeth Englund. San Francisco: Ignatius Press, 1992.
De Lubac, Henri. *Augustinianism and Modern Theology*. Translated by Lancelot Sheppard. New York: The Crossroad Publishing Company New York, 2000.
De Lubac, Henri. *Surnatural*. Paris: Descleé de Brouwer, 1991.
De Lubac, Henri. *The Mystery of the Supernatural*. Translated by Geoffrey Chapman. New York: Crossroad Publishing Company, 1998.
Dulles, Avery. *Models of the Church*. New York: Doubleday & Company, INC., 1974.
Flannery, Austin. *Vatican Council II: The Conciliar and Post Conciliar Documents*. Boston: St. Paul Editions, 1975.
Gallagher, M. P. *Clashing Symbols*. Darton: Longman & Todd, 2003.
Healy, Nicholas J. "Henri de Lubac on Nature and Grace: A Note on Some Recent Contributions to the Debate." *Communio* 35 (Winter 2008): 535-564.
Ireneus, *Adversus Haereses*. Grand Rapids: Wm. B. Eerdmans Publishing, 1989.
Jean-Jacques Rousseau, *On the Social Contract*. Indianapolis: Hackett Publishing Company, 1987.
Jerome. *Letters and Select Works*. Grand Rapids: Wm. B. Eerdmans Publishing, 1954.
John Paul II, *Address to the Pontifical Academy of Social Sciences*, 27 April 2001.
John Paul II. *Ecclesia in Africa*. Vatican City: Libreria Editrice Vaticana, 1995.
John Paul II. *Sollicitudo Rei Sociali*. Vatican City: Libreria Editrice Vaticana, 1987.

Joseph Roger de Benoist, *Léopold Sédar Senghor*. Paris: Beauchesne, 1998.

Katongole, Emmanuel. *The Sacrifice of Africa – A Political Theology for Africa*. Cambridge: Wm. B. Eerdmans Publishing Co., 2011.

Komonchak, Joseph. "Theology and Culture at Mid-Century: The Example of Henri de Lubac." *Theological Studies* 51 (December 1990) 579-602.

Lisa Cahill, "*Caritas in Veritate:* Benedict's Global Reorientation." *Theological Studies*, June 2010; 71, 2.

Maritain, Jacques. *Integral Humanism*. New York: Charles Scribner's Sons, 1968.

Mbeki, Thabo. "*The African Renaissance, South Africa and the World* (Lecture delivered at United Nations University: 9 April 1998).

Meredith, Martin. *The Fate of Africa*. New York: Public Affairs Books, 2005.

Nichols, Aidan. *The Thought of Pope Benedict XVI*. London: Burns and Oates, 2007.

Orobator, Agbonkhianmeghe. "Caritas in Veritate and Africa's Burden of (Under)Development." *Theological Studies*, June 2010; 71, 2.

Philipp Renczes, "Grace Reloaded: Caritas in Veritate's Theological Anthropology." *Theological Studies* 71, June 2010.

Plato. *Republic*. Translated by Benjamin. Jowett. New York: The Dial Press, 1956.

Pontifical Council for Justice and Peace. *Compendium of the Social Doctrine of the Church*. Città del Vaticano: Libreria Editrice Vaticana, 2004.

Pope Francis, Apostolic Blessing – *Urbi et Orbi*. Vatican City: 13 March 2013.

Preface to Constitutions and Rules (Rome: Oblates of Mary Immaculate, 2000.

Ratzinger, Joseph / Pope Benedict XVI *Called to Communion*. Translated by Adrian Walker. San Francisco: Ignatius Press, 1996.

Ratzinger, Joseph / Pope Benedict XVI *Christianity and the Crisis of Cultures*. Translated by Brian McNeil. San Francisco: Ignatius Press, 2006.

Ratzinger, Joseph / Pope Benedict XVI *Church, Ecumenism and Politics*. Translated by Michael J. Miller. San Francisco: Ignatius Press, 2008.

Ratzinger, Joseph / Pope Benedict XVI *Eschatology Death and Eternal Life*. Translated by Michael Waldstein. San Francisco: Ignatius Press, 1988.

Ratzinger, Joseph / Pope Benedict XVI *Europe Today and Tomorrow*. Translated by Michael J. Miller. San Francisco: Ignatius Press, 2007.

Ratzinger, Joseph / Pope Benedict XVI *Introduction to Christianity*. Translated by J. R. Foster. San Francisco: Ignatius Press, 1990.

Ratzinger, Joseph / Pope Benedict XVI *Jesus of Nazareth: Holy Week from the Entrance into Jerusalem to the Resurrection*. Translated by Philip J. Whitmore. San Francisco: Ignatius Press, 2011.

Ratzinger, Joseph / Pope Benedict XVI *Jesus of Nazareth*. Translated by Adrian J. Walker. New York: Doubleday, 2007.

Ratzinger, Joseph / Pope Benedict XVI *Milestones Memoirs 1927-1977*. Translated by Erasmo Leiva-Merikakis. San Francisco: Ignatius Press, 1998.

Ratzinger, Joseph / Pope Benedict XVI *Pilgrim Fellowship of Faith: The Church as Communion*. Translated by Henry Taylor. San Francisco: Ignatius Press, 2005.

Ratzinger, Joseph / Pope Benedict XVI *Principles of Catholic Theology*. Translated by Mary Frances McCarthy. San Francisco: Ignatius Press, 1987.

Ratzinger, Joseph / Pope Benedict XVI *Salt of the Earth*. Translated by Adrian Walker. San Francisco: Ignatius Press, 1997.

Ratzinger, Joseph / Pope Benedict XVI *The Meaning of Christian Brotherhood*. Translated by Sheed and Ward. San Francisco: Ignatius Press, 1966.

Ratzinger, Joseph / Pope Benedict XVI *The Nature and Mission of Theology*. Translated by Adrian Walker. San Francisco: Ignatius Press, 1995.

Ratzinger, Joseph / Pope Benedict XVI *The Spirit of the Liturgy*. Translated by John Saward. San Francisco: Ignatius Press, 2000.

Ratzinger, Joseph / Pope Benedict XVI *The Theology of History in St. Bonaventure*. Translated by Zachary Hayes. Chicago: Franciscan Herald Press, 1989.

Ratzinger, Joseph / Pope Benedict XVI *Theological Highlights of Vatican II*. Translated by Thomas P. Rausch. New York: Paulist Press, 2009.

Ratzinger, Joseph / Pope Benedict XVI *Truth and Tolerance*. Translated by Henry Taylor. San Francisco: Ignatius Press, 2004.

Ratzinger, Joseph / Pope Benedict XVI *Values in a Time of Upheaval*. Translated by Brian McNeil. New York: The Crossroad Publishing Company, 2006.

Ratzinger, Joseph / Pope Benedict XVI. *Biblical Interpretation in Crisis: The Ratzinger Conference on Bible and Church.* Edited by *Richard John Neuhaus.* Grand Rapids: William B. Eerdmans Publishing Company, 1989.

Sanneh, Lamin. *Translating the Message*. New York: Orbis Books, 2009.

Thornton, John and Susan Varenne, *The Essential Pope Benedict XVI: His central writings & speeches*. New York: HarperCollins, 2007.

Turkson, Cardinal Peter K. A. "*Caritas in Veritate:* Good News for Society." *Logos: A Journal of Catholic Thought and Culture*, Volume 15, Number 3, Summer 2012.

Twomey, D. Vincent. *Pope Benedict XVI, The Conscience of Our Age*. San Francisco: Ignatius Press, 2007.

Uelman, Amelia J. "Caritas in Veritate and Chiara Lubich." *Theological Studies*, June 2010; 71, 2.

World Synod of Catholic Bishops. *Justitia in mundo*. Vatican City: Libreria Editrice Vaticana, 1971.

Zamagni, Stefano. *Fraternità, Dono, Reciprocità nella 'Caritas in Veritate'*. Bologna: Università di Bologna, 2009.

INDEX

A New Brotherhood 98-99
Achebe, Chinua 40, 94
Africa and Development 87-89
Africae Munus in relation to *Caritas in Veritate* 85-87
African Stories of Fraternity 93-95
An Analysis of Africa's Commitment (Africae Munus) 72-76
Anthropology 81-82

Barankitse, Maggy 95
Benedict's Metaphysical reading of Humanum in relation to Culture 58-61
Bonanni, Sergio 82

Cahill, Lisa 101, 109
Caritas Christi urget nos 27-30
Caritas in the Encyclical 15
Caritas in Veritate in relation to Africa 103-107
Caritas in Veritate in relation to *Populorum Progressio* 15-17
Catholic Social Teachings that supplement Caritas in Veritate 68-69
Christ as Recapitulation 64-65
Christiansen, Drew 15 101-2
Christology 76-77
Chullo, Stan 35, 37
Church *ad extra* 95-96
Church as a Family and a Fraternity 96-98
Cultus Hominis according to Reason and Metaphysics 56-58
Czerney, Michael 70, 101

de Benoist, Joseph Roger 90
de Lubac, Henri 82
Development as Vocation 51-53
Development of Christian Brotherhood 30-32
Difficulty of the Text 101-103
Dulles, Avery 79-80

Ecclesiology 77-79
Enlightenment of Reason that comes from Christian Revelation 61-62
Eschatology 82-83
Existus-Reditus in the Understanding of Development 66-68

Fraternitas as Charity and Solidarity 53-55
Fraternitas at the core of the Encyclical 100-101
Fraternitas at the Core of the Understanding of Development 65-66
Fraternitas et Communio 36-39
Fraternitas et Gratia 32-33
Fraternitas et Solidarietas 46-48
Fraternitas et Subsidiaritas 42-44
Fraternitas in Societas 45-46
Fundamental Principles of Charity and Truth 17-21

Gallagher, Michael Paul 90
Globalization and Culture 40-42
God as Love 62-63
God as Triune 63-64

Human Community as a Fraternal Community 21-24

Inculturation 89-93
Irenaeus of Lyon 81-2

Jesus 2, 9, 14, 19, 22-3, 30-2, 34, 37, 47, 50, 64, 67, 76, 83, 87, 95, 99-100, 109
John the Beloved 11

Katongole, Emmanuel 41, 94-6
Kierkegaard, Søren 5-6, 15, 112

Lazarus 37
Logic of Gift 48-50

Logos of God 34-35
Luke 37-8

Marimion, Columba 60
Maritain, Jacques 8-11
Marx, Karl 27-8
Mbeki, Thabo 93-4
Meredith, Martin 75-6, 91

Orobator, Agbonkhianmeghe 78, 103-7

Pastoral Perspectives to Development 69-71
Pastoral Theology 83-84
Paul VI and *Fraternitas* as Charity and Solidarity 55-56
Phenomenon of Globalization 39-40
Plato 18, 58
Pliny the Elder 93
Pope Benedict XVI (see: Joseph Ratzinger) 1-4, 6-7, 10-17, 20, 25, 28, 33, 36, 57, 60, 65-8, 70, 72, 75-7, 88-9, 92-3, 103, 109, 111-12
Pope Francis 112-13
Pope John Paul II 15-6, 34, 39, 73, 89, 104, 111
Pope Leo XIII 6-7, 111
Pope Paul VI 1, 3, 6-7, 15-7, 19-20, 28, 51, 53-7, 66, 68-9, 73, 88, 100, 104-5, 111
Pope Pius XI 20

Principal Parameters of Mission 99
Purpose of *Caritas in Veritate* 5-9

Ratzinger, Joseph (see: Pope Benedict XVI) 1, 5, 21, 27, 30-1, 38, 47, 52, 54, 65-7, 74, 88-9, 92, 100, 105, 108-11

Relationship between Church and State 108-111
Renczes, Philipp 32
Rosanna 70
Rousseau, Jean-Jacques 110

Sacramentology 79-81
Senghor, Léopald Sédar 89-90
St. Augustine 38, 41-2, 56, 90, 97-8, 102, 107
St. Basil 99
St. Jerome 82
St. John Chrysostom 37
St. Paul 9, 30, 50, 82

Thornton, John 75, 92
Turkson, Peter 69-70, 101

Uelman, Amelia J. 103
Understanding of Fraternitas 25-27

Varenne, Susan 75, 92

Zamagni, Stefano 43, 46-7, 49-50

About the Author

IZRAEL THABANG NKADIMENG is a Catholic priest based in Washington, DC, and a systematic theologian. He was born in Johannesburg, South Africa, and, in addition to English, Italian, and French, is fluent in several other languages. He holds degrees from the Pontifical Gregorian University in Rome and the Catholic University of America in Washington, DC. He also holds diplomas from St. Joseph's Theological Institute in South Africa and the Catholic University of Paris in France.

Father Nkadimeng is a member of various research organizations, including the Francesco Collaborative, which seeks to implement the principles of Catholic Social Teaching, especially concerning investments. His other research interests include the Church Fathers and the Second Vatican Council.

FUORI COLLANA

The books in this series are of subject matter related to things Italian and/or Italian/American though not always in a direct manner. Hence, this "out-of-network" series allows Casa Lago Press *to include subject matter that is "indirectly" related to its main mission.*

Anthony Julian Tamburri. *A Politics of [Self-]Omission: The Italian/American Knowledge in a Post-George Floyd Age.* ISBN 978-1-955995-50-7. 2025. Originally published in Italy by Aracne in 2022.

CASA LAGO PRESS EDITORIAL GROUP

David Aliano
Leonardo Buonomo
William Boelhower
Ryan Calabretta-Sajder
Nancy Carnevale
Stephen J. Cerulli
Donna Chirico
Fred Gardaphé
Paolo A. Giordano
Nicolas Grosso

Donatella Izzo
John Kirby
Chiara Mazzucchelli
Emanuele Pettener
Mark Pietralunga
Joseph Sciorra
Ilaria Serra
Anthony Julian Tamburri
Sabrina Vellucci
Leslie Wilson

www.ingramcontent.com/pod-product-compliance
Lightning Source LLC
Chambersburg PA
CBHW020939090426
42736CB00010B/1194